Classic Cocktails

In the same series:

Classic Rum
Julie Arkell

Classic Vodka
Nicholas Faith & Ian Wisniewski

Classic Blended Scotch
Jim Murray

Classic Bourbon Tennessee & Rye
Jim Murray

Classic Irish Whiskey
Jim Murray

Classic Bottled Beers of the World
Roger Protz

Classic Stout & Porter
Roger Protz

Classic Tequila
Ian Wisniewski

Classic Cocktails

Salvatore Calabrese

To Sue, thank you for your support and patience

First published in Great Britain in 1997 by PRION BOOKS
32-34 Gordon House Road London NW5 1LP

Reprinted 1997 and 1998

Editorial coordination by Lynn Bryan
Designed by Jill Plank
Cocktail photography by James Duncan

A CIP catalogue record for this book is available from the British Library.
ISBN 1-85375-240-1

Printed and bound in China by Sino Publishing

Contents

Hi-Ti-Hi
Polka
Founded on the
Very Successful Songs
"Hi-Tiddley-Hi-Ti"
& Where did you get that Hat
Clicqu
By
Warwick Williams.

INTRODUCTION

MAKING A COCKTAIL IS AN ART, LIKE THEATRE. A BAR IS THE STAGE FOR MANY PERFORMANCES, NOT ONLY THE BARTENDER'S, BUT ALSO THE CUSTOMERS IN THE BAR. THE BARTENDER IS DOCTOR, PSYCHOLOGIST AND PSYCHIATRIST IN ONE.

He is everybody's best friend and a shoulder to cry on. To be a bartender is to practise the art of conviviality and humanity to all types of people at all social levels.

A sense of romance and of intrigue surrounds the word "cocktail" – it conjures up images of smoky Speakeasies, gangster Al Capone and his associates and beautiful women dressed in slinky satin and silk gowns. Of gravel-voiced sirens crooning Cole Porter tunes. Every movement in these places watched and pre-empted by the Bartender.

Many of the cocktails in this book were created by legendary bartenders who, perhaps, did not imagine the drinks they concocted would be as well known as they are now. They would put together all kinds of combinations from whatever they could find to make the taste of the Prohibition bathtub spirit palatable. Seventy per cent of the cocktails ordered across

Opposite
The cocktail has always provided inspiration for the songwriter. Cole Porter once managed to rhyme "fountain of youth" with "gin and vermouth".

the bar these days are those created during Prohibition, from the champagne cocktails to the Mai Tai. It is hard to beat the mystique of these drinks. That period in drink history made an everlasting impact on our psychological taste buds...the thrill of secretiveness, of drinking illegal substances, is somehow retained in the cocktail itself... the Martini, the Manhattan and the Jack Rose. To sip these illicit nectars is to be transported back into the forbidden glamour of the speakeasy.

The 1920s, 30s and 40s were the decades of the new drink – these were mainly short and mainly alcoholic. Even if a split was added, the spirit made up the majority of the drink. The aim was a quick hit. Shorts were ordered by drinkers who didn't want the same glass in front of them for too long. The use of splits and fruit juices was minimal.

Now, most drinks are long and alcohol is the minority ingredient. People are choosing the drink for refreshment and for the pleasure of the drink as they sit and relax.

To me, a cocktail must satisfy the eyes, satisfy the nose and, thirdly, satisfy the palate. The perfect cocktail is a crescendo of three elements – colour, flavour and texture. There is an enormous pleasure in creating a new drink, in achieving the balance between sweetness and sharpness. The key is to use ingredients that will not "fight" each other. The popularity of the newer fruit juices has inspired many of the new drinks. I focus on the flavour of the fruit juice, then think about what other ingredients it will combine with. The juice inspires the colour – a combination of colours is important in a long drink. Also, when you create a drink you have to give it an appropriate name, one that will be remembered for some years.

One hundred of the cocktails in this book are established classics; ten are my own recipes which I have created for competitions, colleagues, guests and friends. I have included a few secrets of my own that you might find useful, as well as information about equipment, measures, spirit and fruit juice ingredients. All in all, a spirited concoction that makes the most delicious cocktail. Enjoy!

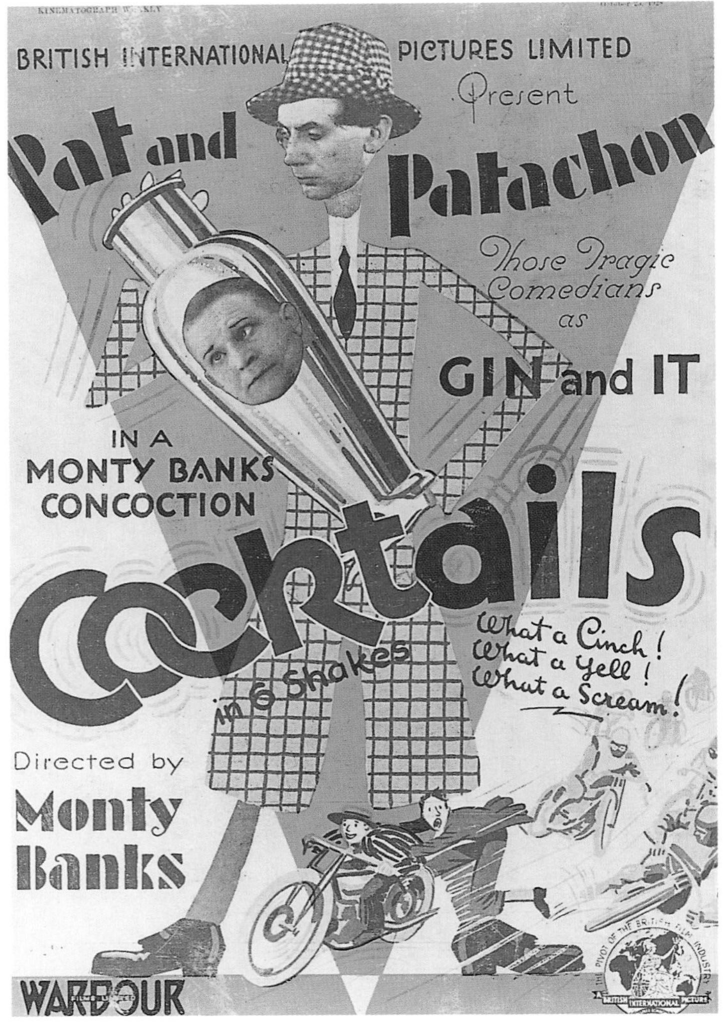
BRITISH INTERNATIONAL PICTURES LIMITED
Present
Pat and Patachon
Those Tragic Comedians as
GIN and IT
IN A MONTY BANKS CONCOCTION
Cocktails
in 6 Shakes
What a Cinch!
What a Yell!
What a Scream!
Directed by
Monty Banks
WARDOUR
THE PIVOT OF THE BRITISH FILM INDUSTRY
A BRITISH INTERNATIONAL PICTURE

THE WORD

JUST EXACTLY WHERE THE WORD "COCKTAIL" ORIGINATED IS STILL A MYSTERY. THERE ARE A GOOD MANY LEGENDS, BUT FEW FACTS. SOME OF THEM ARE A LITTLE FAR-FETCHED BUT I HAVE INCLUDED THEM IN THIS SECTION FOR YOUR AMUSEMENT.

There is little doubt that the word originated in America. An early mention of the word can be found in an American publication, *Balance and Columbian Repository*, dated 13 May, 1806: "A 'Cocktail' is a stimulating liquor composed of spirits of any kind, sugar, water, and bitters, it is vulgarly called bittered sling ...".

Opposite
Monty Banks' Cocktails in 6 Shakes *– alcohol has always been a catalyst for on screen drama.*

Certainly over 100 years ago the word was an accepted description for mixed drinks and the commercially manufactured mixes that were already popular in most of the United States in the 19th century.

In *The Cocktail Book – A Sideboard Manual for Gentlemen* (John MacQueen, 1933) is the delightful legend of the "Cock's Tail" and of a young lady, Daisy, credited with its origin. During the American War of Independence the publican of The Bunch of Grapes inn, Squire Allen, was a fan of cock-fighting. One day he discovered the loss of his finest bird and was bereft. Some time later, a young lieutenant came riding into town with the fine cock under his arm. The Squire was overjoyed at its return and ordered Daisy to provide the young man with the finest refreshment. The young Daisy mixed "sundry drops of bitters and wine of roots with a dram of good Kentucky whiskey, the whole poured over some generous bits of ice and they all drank of the beverage 'to the cock's tail' – for Jupiter (the cockerel) had not lost a single feather."

The gallant Lieutenant swore that, in memory of the event, the drink should be known in the Army as a "cock's tail".

And who are we to disagree?

Another version tells of a tavern owner of the same period who refused to allow his daughter Bessie to marry an American officer. His prize cockerel disappeared, causing him to offer his daughter's hand in marriage to whosoever returned the bird. There are no prizes for guessing who found the bird. The rejected officer – and Bessie's father kept his promise. Bessie made a mixture of drinks from various bottles on the bar shelf during the celebration which the guests thought delicious and consequently the drinks became cocktails.

Yet another tale attributes the term to one of George Washington's officers who proposed a toast to the Yankee general's feathered cap with the words:

"A toast to the cock's tail".

The term "cock-tailed" was a racing term used around 1769 to describe a non-thoroughbred horse. The tails of these animals were docked making it look like the tail of a cockerel. Hence, a "cock-tailed" horse was one of mixed blood. This reference is listed in the *Oxford English Dictionary*, which also states that the word pertains to a person acting like a gentleman but not having the true breeding of one.

There is also an old expression "cocked tail" used to describe a horse or person of high spirits – a drink to raise people's spirits would thus be called "a cocktail".

Cock-ale, fed to fighting cocks in training in the 18th century, contained spirits. Spectators would drink a similar mixture in a toast to the cock with the most feathers left in his tail – the number of spirits were the same as the number of feathers.

The French too have claimed quite a few links to derivation of the word. The French word for egg cup is "coquetier" and a Monsieur Antoine Peychaud, a New Orleans chemist, is reported to have served mixed drinks to his guests in egg cups. The drinks became known as coquetiers .

An old French recipe which contained a concoction of wines, "coquetel", was taken to America by General Lafayette in 1777. Two years later, a Betsy Flanagan of Virginia served soldiers a drink with all the colours of a cock's tail – and the soldiers named it "cock tail".

Another version of the Betsy Flanagan story claims she was the widow of a Revolutionary soldier who kept a tavern visited by the French. Her neighbour was a loyalist and she purloined a few of his fowl to feed the French. The pre-dinner mixed drinks were decorated with tail feathers from these prized cocks and the group of merry soldiers toasted her with the words: "Vive le cock-tail".

The late and knowledgeable bartender Harry Craddock was adamant that all of the legends involving the cock's tail as the origin of the word cocktail are incorrect. He believed the true origin of the word can be traced back to an incident at the beginning of the 19th century:

The American Army of the Southern States had been in skirmishes with King Axolotl VIII of Mexico. A truce was called and both leaders agreed to meet at the King's Pavilion. King Axolotl asked if the General would like a drink and a young lady appeared, carrying just one cup containing a strange potion she had brewed. A hush fell over the assembled dignitaries – there was only one cup and either the King or the General would have to drink from it first, and the other would be insulted. The young lady realised this, bowed to the gathering and drank the drink herself. The situation was saved. Before leaving, the General asked for the young lady's name. The King is alleged to have replied that it was his daughter, Coctel. Thus, Coctel became "cocktail".

Upon publication of this tale, Harry Craddock received a letter from one Lucas de Palacio disputing this story. According to his version, English sailors went ashore at Campeche on the Yucatan Peninsula, Mexico, and quenched their thirst at the city's taverns. In those days, drinks were served without mixing. Sometimes a "drac" was ordered – this was a mixture of liquors slowly stirred with (usually) a wooden spoon. In one of these taverns, a lad stirred the drinks not with a spoon but the root of a plant, called "Cola de Gallo" – in English, the cock's tail. The sailors asked what the lad was using to stir their drinks. He replied: "Cola de Gallo". The word became common usage in Campeche as sailors asked not for dracs, but for cocktails.

With the word came the ritual – the mixing of the (strong) liquors, the occasion of its drinking (triumph over adversity) conferring an unspoken sophistication upon the drinker. For the cocktail was not a mere tankard of ale, not a short shot of one pure spirit. The cocktail showed that the drinker had a refined palate and appreciated the subtle chemistry of the alcoholic ingredients.

The first cocktail book – *The Bon Vivant's Guide, or How to Mix Drinks* – was published in the 1860s by legendary bartender "Professor" Jerry Thomas, and it has been followed by many others. Harry Johnson's *Illustrated Bartenders' Manual* was another landmark. Published in 1882, it featured an illustration of

an ice-filled bar glass with an inverted metal cone...the precursor to what we now know as the modern cocktail shaker.

Many of the world's favourite cocktails were invented before the 20th century had begun – the Mint Julep, the Daiquiri, the Gin Fizz, the Corpse Reviver – and the Martini. But most owed their origins to the roaring twenties.

Opposite
The mythic speakeasy was a place where social inhibitions dissolved in the sparkling maelstrom of the bootleg cocktail.

THE EFFECT OF PROHIBITION

The drinking habits of Americans changed abruptly with the introduction of Prohibition on January 17, 1920. The Volstead Act stated it was illegal to sell, manufacture, deliver or trade in alcohol. What the Act did was drive the drinkers behind closed doors; it created secret societies with a special knock as their password to inebriation. The very illicitness of it all made the cocktail twice as alluring, twice as delectable. It irrevocably altered the way that Americans drank. This was a society where, prior to 1914, the host did not serve pre-dinner drinks. Now, because alcohol was forbidden, couples went out of their domesticity in search of a pre-dinner, a pre-theatre drink. No longer were bars places for boys alone; wives and mistresses were taken to Speakeasies – perhaps to add respectability to the illicitness?

The era of Prohibition was ironically one of unadulterated hedonism. The Jazz Age, as the

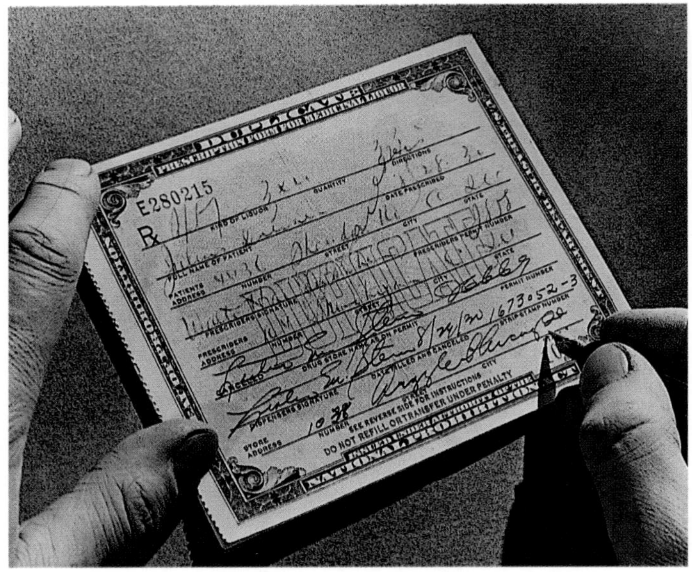

writer F. Scott Fitzgerald called it, was a time when women were liberated from the home and reborn in the image of the flapper – an independent, leisured girl who threw her cares to the wind and lived indulgently for the moment. The sexual image of the flapper dominated the 1920s and, to many people, the cocktail was the liquid embodiment of that pleasure principle. The names of cocktails revelled in sensuality and innuendo: Bosom Caresser, Atta Boy, Knickerbocker, Parisian Blonde, One Exciting Night and Temptation. The Angels' Tit, topped off by a cherry nipple, even looked as if it were that of an angel.

Opposite
A prescription form for medicinal liquor – one of the many ingenious ways of getting a fix of the hard stuff during Prohibiton.

Cocktails were also named after Parisian streets – Saint-Germain; automobiles – Rolls Royce, and even film stars – the Marilyn Monroe is a champagne cocktail named after the blonde star because Dom Perignon was her favourite champagne. Angels were omnipresent – Angels' Kiss, Fallen Angel, Angel Face; and animals – the Moscow Mule, Mule's Hind Leg (drinks with a kick), Monkey Gland and Leap Frog. Others were just plain silly – Whizz Doodle, Whizz Bang, XYZ Cocktail and Zed.

Prohibition's long-term effect was to create organized crime, bribery and corruption at local and national levels. It made a national hero of gangster Al Capone – the original bootlegger ("Bootlegging" refers to the practise of smuggling whiskey inside the boot). The word "moonshine" also became part of our vocabulary as a result of illicit stills working under the pale light of the moon. Capone became a focal point for Prohibition outrage, but he also became a rich and powerful man, as did many others – among them the late John F. Kennedy's father, Joe Kennedy.

Throughout the 1920s and 30s the cocktail maintained its dazzling allure. Glamour was cool and hedonism rife – it was party time in America. Nightclubs mushroomed all over New York – The Stork Club, El Morocco, The Knickerbocker Grill, Park Avenue Club, Morgan's – and in hedonistic Hollywood. These bars were places to be seen, to listen to

Above
The Cotton Club in Harlem.
Opposite
During Prohibition, gay Paris was the place Americans went when they wanted a real drink and a good time.

jazz players' latest tunes. Club owners became celebrities in their own right. Private parties were awash with bathtub gin, usually disguised as the Martini. By 1929, there were over 120 recipes in existence.

The American rich went to Europe when they felt like a drink in public and they took the cocktail with them. The phenomenon boomed in Paris and London during Prohibition. Harry's New York Bar in Paris and The American Bar at The Savoy in London built up their reputations around the magic of the cocktail. Bartenders created drinks for any occasion. After Prohibition, the social habits remained. This was the era of the cocktail pianist, the female cocktail singer whose voice was like liquid velvet, pouring sensuality over the troubles of the day. A potent mix of sex, sin and spirits. The celebrity lifestyle was firmly

Postcards From Paris

Making a Peach Cordial

We asked for these!!

Australian Virgin
Dizzy Blonde
Fuzzy Navel
Hen Night
Love in the Afternoon
Menage à Trois
Mistress
Screaming Orgasm
Sex on the Beach
Slow Comfortable Screw
The Shooter
Zipper Ripper

entrenched and remained so until America's entry into World War Two.

When Prohibition ended in 1933, the style of the cocktail bar changed. Gone were the small and intimate darkened bars. The liquor business was in an expansive mood. It was the era of the big band and big entertainment rooms. The swank New York club, The Rainbow Room, opened in 1934 as a direct response to the demand for sophisticated drinks, music and dancing. Bars were places to meet and be seen. Drink underwent a subtle metamorphosis – the short cocktail took second place to the highball. All that dancing required refreshment.

Hollywood also embraced the cocktail with a passion. Writers created scenes whereby the Martini was the central prop – no doubt a reflection of their own lives. Champagne cocktails, Old-fashioneds, Manhattans – screen dialogue was splattered with cocktail orders at the bar. The cocktail, in screen language, gave women power and the films of the 20s and 30s explored this new relationship. Screen sirens sipped seductively and plotted while staring into the eyes of the handsome leading man.

World War Two was the death knell for such spacious bars devoted to frivolity. Only the smaller, more intimate bars survived since most men of a drinking age had gone to war.

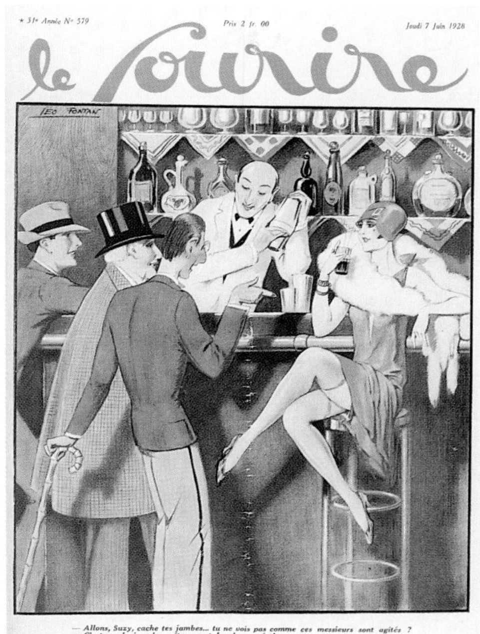

Left
The cover of the French magazine Le Sourire, *1928, drawn by Leo Fontan.*

The 1950s was a time of rebuilding the family unit and of consolidation after the economic effects of the war. Then came the decade of the 1960s and overnight everything changed. The Brandy Alexander – a mixture of brandy, crême de cacao and cream – was to be the bridging drink between teenage years and adulthood for many chic young women. Yet this was the era of rebellion against tradition and for many young people it was flower-power, drugs and rock 'n' roll and not the cocktail lounge that dominated their external social behaviour. The revolution in popular music that began with Elvis, moved on rapidly with The Beatles, The Byrds and Bob Dylan, and ended in the 70s with the discotheque. After a few hours in this maelstrom of lights, heat and body-threshing, you needed a drink quickly, and the drink had to be thirst-quenching and refreshing. Less alcoholic. The elegance of the cocktail had slipped through our little fingers.

There was also the phenomenon of the wine bar. Throughout this dark period, only the top-class hotel provided a haven for the sophisticated cocktail imbiber. Here, a person knew they could slip onto the padded bar stool, look the bartender in the eye and ask for a Sidecar and not be mocked.

The 1980s saw a revival of the classic cocktail and a renewed interest by the large spirit-producing companies in luring the younger generation into drinking more spirits. The image given to cocktails for today's young is quite different from that of the sophisticated 1920s, reflecting the trend towards drinks that are colourful, exotic and fun to drink. More juices, more refreshment.

There is no doubt that the cocktail is making a strong come-back. The Martini is still the most revered cocktail, a refined drink for the connoisseur. Other exotic drinks, such as the daiquiri and the margarita, are strong-sellers, perhaps because they remind patrons of

Left
Cast your troubles away – a 1930s advertisement for Bols.

happier, sunshine days. When an economy is in a rut, the population takes to living out its fantasies.

There is also something in the search for a new, delicious experience for the palate. As our knowledge of food has grown so has the interest in wine and spirits. The cocktail is an essential part of this social history of food and drink. A boredom threshold has been reached with wine – asking for a glass of chablis or chardonnay no longer holds the status it did. For those who want an exotic experience for their palates, there is, and always will be, the cocktail.

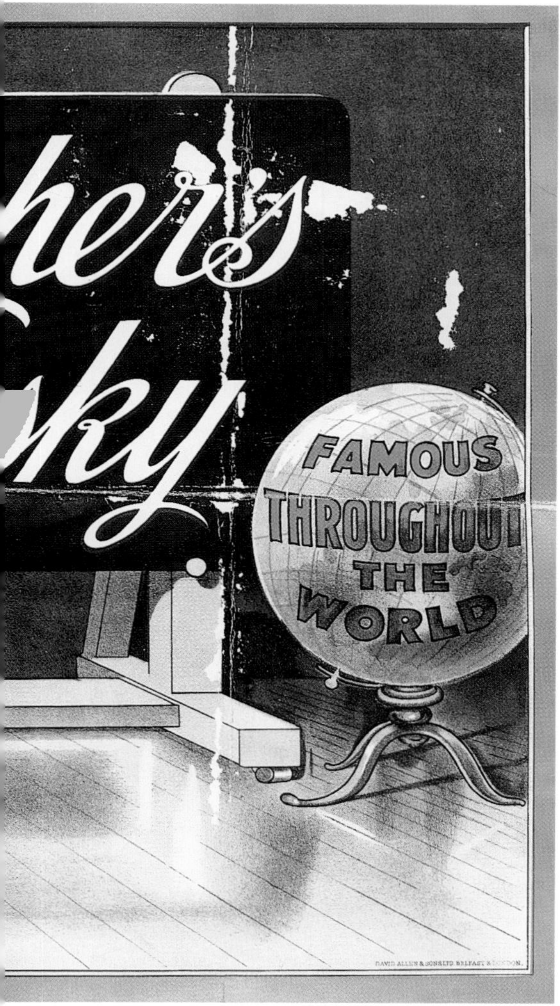

Left
After the Volstead Act, Teacher's was exported to Canada and smuggled into the USA. As a result it was well known there by the time Prohibition was repealed and continued to fill cocktail glasses across the States.

Cocktail Essentials

From the moment the spirit bottles are lined up on the bar, the splits placed in the fridge to chill and the ice is packed away in the freezer, the scene is set for a successful party. So what else do you need? Read on and I'll tell you.

Setting up the bar is as important as mixing the drink. As in all things – preparation is important. Many of the stock items you need are in the kitchen cupboards, so you will not have to go to extra expense. It is essential to lay everything out neatly, and to keep your bar utensils clean.

Opposite
The well-equipped bar is a happy bar.

Ice: An ample supply of ice cubes and/or crushed ice is essential when having people for cocktails. ***Never use the same ice twice.***

Fresh fruit juice: Squeeze just prior to the occasion and keep in the refrigerator. If only making cocktails for two, squeeze when required. The fresher the juice, the better the cocktail will taste.

Cutting a twist: Cut the citrus rind (peel) as thin as possible and about 3 1/2cm (1 1/4in) long.

BAR STOCK

Base spirits

Gin
Brandy
Vodka
Rum – light and dark
Tequila
Scotch whisky
Bourbon whiskey
Dry vermouth
Sweet vermouth
Cointreau / triple sec
Crême de menthe
Kummel
Advocaat
Crême de cassis
Kahlua or Tia Maria
Sherry
Tawny port
Champagne

Fresh Fruit

Lemons
Limes
Oranges
Pineapples

Garnishes

Maraschino cherries
Green cocktail olives
Strawberries (in season)
Celery stalks
Sprigs of fresh mint
Oranges, lemons and limes

Decoration of a cocktail is a personal matter. A garnish should be simple, edible and balance the flavour of the drink. Elegance is the key. For example, with a strawberry daiquiri, all you need is a single fresh strawberry.

Sugar, Syrups and Sweeteners
Cubed sugar
Caster sugar (superfine)
Grenadine syrup
Gomme syrup

You can make your own sugar syrup (gomme syrup) by pouring 250g (1lb)granulated sugar into 1 cup of hot water. Boil, skim and cool, then pour into bottles. Store in a cool place.

Grenadine syrup is made from pomegranates and gives a cocktail colour, from pink to deep red, as well as a sweet taste.

Mixers and Fruit Juices

Soda water
Cola
Tonic
Dry ginger ale
Lemonade /Seven Up
Bitter lemon
Lime juice cordial
Peppermint cordial
Angostura bitters *
Coconut cream
Pineapple juice
Tomato juice

* Originally a medicinal drink to stimulate the metabolism, bitters are a mixture of herbs, roots and other botanicals. Angostura has over 40 ingredients which include gentian root.

Spices and seasoning

Fresh nutmeg for grating
Celery salt
Salt
Black pepper
Tabasco
Olive oil
Worcestershire sauce

Equipment

- Bar knife
- Bar spoon
- Bar tongs
- Black pepper mill
- Blender
- Bottle opener
- Can opener
- Corkscrew
- Cutting board
- Champagne stopper
- Cocktail napkins
- Cocktail sticks
- Cocktail stirrers
- Fruit juice jug
- Fruit squeezer
- Glass-cleaning cloth
- Grater
- Ice bucket
- Ice scoop
- Ice tongs
- Mixing glass
- Shaker – three-piece or Boston shaker
- Spirit measure
- Straws
- Tray
- Wooden muddler

Glassware

- Brandy balloon
- Champagne flute
- Cocktail glass
- Highball glass
- Hot drink glass (for Irish coffee, hot toddy)
- Liqueur glass
- Medium-sized wine goblet
- Old-fashioned glass
- Piña colada glass/ large goblet
- Port or sherry glass

A glass with a fine rim for the lips to touch, a slender stem (when appropriate) for the hand to balance, and a harmony with the drink it holds – these are the three essential points to look for when choosing your glassware.

Cocktail Terms

Aperitif A dry to medium drink served before dinner to stimulate, or anaesthetise, the appetite.

Build To pour the ingredients directly into the glass. Add ice only if required by the recipe.

Dash A splash, a tiny amount.

Digestif A smooth, balanced, fairly sweet drink served after dinner.

Float A tiny amount of liquor poured very carefully on the top of a cocktail.

Mix To pour the ingredients into the cone of an electric drink mixer, and mix. Then strain into the appropriate glass.

Muddle Muddling involves mashing or grinding herbs such as mint to a smooth paste in the bottom of a glass. A wooden muddler is best as it does not scratch the glass.

Neat Served with no ice and not mixed.

On The Rocks Poured over ice.

Shake To pour the ingredients into a cocktail shaker with ice.

Spiral A peel of fruit cut in a spiral way, used either in the drink or as a garnish.

Stir Put ice into a mixing glass, add the ingredients, stir for about 10 seconds until chilled and then pour into the appropriate glass.

Straight up A drink that is mixed and served without ice.

Twist A longish strip of peel twisted in the middle and dropped into the drink.

Liqueurs used in Recipes

Advocaat	Made from egg yolks and grape brandy.
Absinthe	Strong, dry, bitter, high-alcohol liqueur made from anise seed and wormwood. Was linked with mental illness and banned since 1910s.
Applejack	Apple brandy made in USA.
Amaretto	Almond- and apricot- flavoured liqueur from Italy.
Benedictine	One of the oldest, if not the oldest, golden liqueur made from various herbs, concocted by Benedictine monks as far back as 1510.
Cachaça	Aguardente de Cana, a sugar cane spirit, is distilled from concentrated and fermented sugar cane sap.
Calvados	Apple brandy made in France from fermented apple juice and aged in oak casks.
Cherry brandy	Produced by maceration of the fruit in spirit, sometimes with the addition of herbs.
Cointreau	Orange-flavoured liqueur made by the French Cointreau family since 1849.
Crême de cassis	Blackcurrant liqueur.
Crême de menthe	White or green liqueur made from a concentrate of mint leaves.
Crême de cacao	Chocolate-flavoured liqueur distilled from cocoa beans (and sometimes vanilla) macerated in alcohol, diluted and sweetened. White has a more subtle flavour and is clear.
Curaçao	Sweet orange-flavoured liqueur. Often substituted for Cointreau.
Drambuie	Oldest of the whisky liqueurs made with heather, honey and herbs.

Galliano Italian liqueur made from over 80 herbs, with aniseed dominant.

Grand Marnier French Curaçao created in 1880 with a cognac base.

Kahlua Mexican coffee liqueur.

Kummel Spearmint-flavoured liqueur.

Maraschino White Italian liqueur made from the distillation of sour Marasca cherries. Sometimes a dash of kirsch is added.

Orgeat Almond-flavoured syrup.

Pernod Concentrated aniseed-flavoured liqueur that turns white when water is added.

Tia Maria Jamaican rum-based liqueur flavoured with Blue Mountain coffee extract and spices.

Triple sec A sweet white Curaçao.

Right
An early 20th-century advertisement for absinthe, the allegedly mind-bending tipple of Bohemian café society. Banned during World War I, because of its feared links with mental illness, absinthe distillers such as Pernod began producing anise as a substitute.

OT ABSINTHE
-LEM-
errot !!!

Tips and Techniques

- A chilled glass is essential for a cocktail. Either place the glasses in the freezer for half an hour before use, or fill each glass with crushed ice just before use. Throw away the crushed ice when you make the drink.

- To frost a glass: put the glass in a refrigerator or bury it in shaved ice for long enough to give a frosted finish to the glass. The glass should look ice-cold and feel very cold.

- To give the glass a sugar-frosted look, dampen the rim of a pre-chilled glass with a slice of lemon or lime and dip the rim into a saucer of caster sugar.

- Handle any glass by the bottom of the glass or by the stem (i.e., a cocktail glass).

- For drinks served with a mixer, use a highball glass. Always fill the glass two-thirds full of ice, then add the ingredients.

- Use the cheapest ingredients first. If you make a mistake, you have wasted less money.

- Shake a mixture of egg, fruit juice or syrup so that it is almost frozen whilst the ingredients are combined. Shake for 8–10 seconds. If using cream, shake more sharply.

- Do not shake a fizzy drink.

- An egg white, when combined with other ingredients and shaken, will give otherwise clear drinks a smooth look and a white frothy head. The egg white is tasteless.

- Use a mixing glass for cocktails containing only alcoholic products.

- Use an electric blender for recipes that require fresh fruits and cream and which use crushed ice. First put in the solid ingredients, blend quickly on low speed for about 8–10 seconds. Then add crushed ice and blend on high speed for five seconds. Adding the crushed ice last allows the fruit to liquidise without too much dilution. Pour and serve the drink immediately.

- Still or sparkling mineral waters should be served chilled, without ice unless requested. Add a wedge of lime or lemon.

- Serve a cocktail immediately as it will separate if you leave it to stand.

TRY A
BIG 4
COCKTAIL
ROCHER
DIGESTIF

GREAT BARTENDERS

"Professor" Jerry Thomas Cocktail pioneer and the man who created the Blue Blazer and the Tom & Jerry. He became famous during the 1850s and 60s, especially when bartender at the Metropolitan Hotel, New York. When he toured Europe, he travelled with his set of sterling silver mixing cups (the precursor to shakers) from which, when he was mixing the Blue Blazer, trailed a flame of liquid.

Harry Craddock Bartender at The Savoy, London from 1920 until 1939. Known for his charming personality, Harry was the first President of the United Kingdom Bartenders Guild and introduced many American cocktails to Europe. The American Bar at The Savoy was often referred to as the 49th State during his tenure and it was definitely the place to drink.

Victor Bergeron Familiarly known as "Trader" Vic who, in the 1930s, opened Hinky Dinks, a bar in Oakland, California, with a "huntin' and shootin'" theme. He changed this to a Pacific Island theme bar, with masks and conch shells, and created drinks such as Dr Funk of Tahiti, The Suffering Bastard and the White Witch.

Opposite
"Try a Big 4 Cocktail" – rye whiskey for the US, Scotch for Great Britain, Noilly Prat for France and vodka for the Soviet Union. The answer to the world's problems is shaken by bartender Emile, watched by Harry MacElhone owner of Harry's New York Bar in Paris, 1949.

Opposite above
The London Savoy bar in the 1930s.
Opposite below
Johnny Brooks at work in his bar at The Stork Club, New York.

Johnny Brooks An American bartender who was famous not only for his charm and great personality, but also for the Martini with a twist of lemon that he served at the Stork Club, New York throughout the 1940s. The club was a favourite watering-hole of film stars such as Marlene Dietrich (who liked men who liked Martinis) and writers such as Ernest Hemingway.

Don Beach The bartender who created the Zombie at his Don the Beachcomber restaurant, Hollywood, in 1934, as well as another 63 exotic cocktails. His Pacific island-themed restaurants and bars were highly successful.

Giuseppe Cipriani Creator of the Bellini, a champagne and fresh peach juice cocktail, in 1943 at Harry's Bar, Venice.

Fernand "Pete" Petiot Created the Bloody Mary at Harry's Bar, Paris in 1921. He later moved to the King Cole Grill at the St Regis Hotel, New York.

THE COCKTAIL SHAKER

When a monogrammed silver cocktail shaker once owned by the late John F. Kennedy, (and auctioned as part of the estate of his late widow, Jackie Onassis) can fetch $23,000, you know there's reason to be all shook up.

There are four cocktail shakers from the Art Deco period on permanent display in the Museum of Modern Art, New York. As we approach the millennium, department stores report that sales of cocktail shakers and glasses are overtaking sales of tea sets – a traditional wedding list gift.

In 1520, the intrepid conquistador, Cortez, wrote in his despatches of a "frothy and foaming" drink, made with cacao, and served from a gold cylinder-shaped container. Could this have been the model for modern cocktail shakers?

The idea of a shaker was first enacted by an innkeeper who, while pouring the mixture for a drink back and forth between two containers, discovered the smaller rim fitted into the larger. He held the two containers together and shook. The US Patent Office records reveal an application for a patent for "improvements in apparatus for mixing drinks" was approved in 1872.

Right
One of the rarest shakers today is that in the shape of a penguin, designed in 1936, and sold in its day for $20. Its hinged beak lifts to reveal a pouring spout. It is such ingenuity which makes these novelty shakers collectible.

Above
A pepperpot in the style of a cocktail shaker is seen next to a British 50-pence piece.
Opposite
Two cocktail shakers in the shape of lighthouses and one in the shape of a yachting buoy.

There are more developments dated 1877 and 1881. By 1886 the Meriden Britannia Company (now the American International Silver Company) catalogue featured 12 pages of barware, including six sizes of the two-piece cocktail shaker.

By the late 19th century the cocktail shaker was the standard tool of the bartender. The London department store, Harrods, featured two silver-plated cocktail shakers in their 1908 catalogue, priced at four shillings and ninepence and five shillings and ninepence. These were advertised as being "for mixing American drinks".

In 1928, the respected American industrial designer Lurelle Guild designed two cocktail

serving sets in the style of skyscrapers. The streamlined silver-plated Manhattan shakers were manufactured by the Wilcox Silver Plate Co. and are sought-after collector's items. Meriden's 1929 catalogue featured a silver-plated set with a hand-chased grape-leaf design shaker in a teapot style. For the modern-minded, there was a rooster in an Art Deco motif, silver-plated lighthouses and golf bags. Many "standard" designs were made of high-tech materials and mass-produced: for example, chrome-plated stainless steel with a Bakelite handle. These were non-tarnishing items and did not require polishing. Glass manufacturers produced etched designs in brilliant hues of ruby red, green and cobalt blue.

Novelty shakers were popular throughout the 1930s – glass shakers featured pink elephants and stylised cockerels; silver-plated zeppelins, aeroplanes, lighthouses and milk churns were seen in the best cocktail cabinets. The Second World War ended the production of metal shakers since all metal was required for the American war effort.

After the war, technology had progressed and electrical goods dominated the kitchen. The 1950s decade was a push-button era for drink dispensers, and the electric blender took the place of the shaker. Take several cubes of ice, add alcohol, flick a switch and – instant drink! It was farewell to the ritual, showmanship, personality and elegance.

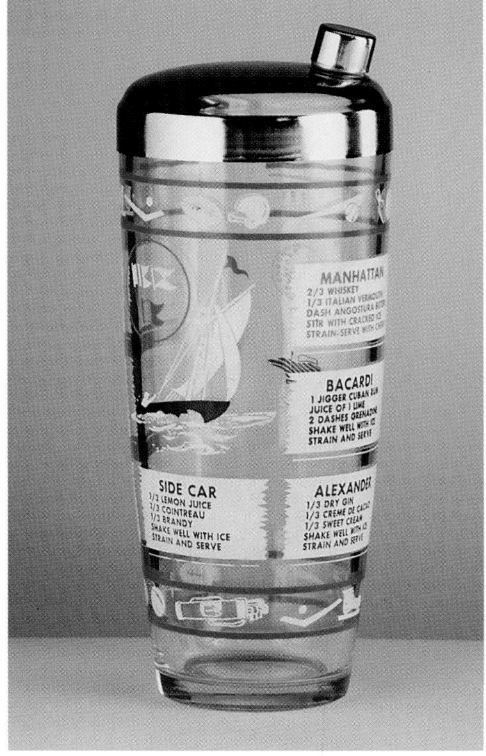

Left
A typical British 1930s enamelled glass shaker with a chrome lid.

The blender was an American invention and its role moved easily from food preparation to mixing drinks, helping to change the taste of cocktails. It meant pieces of fruit and thicker juices could be added to alcohol. Drinks became longer, colourful and textural. Now, a blender is as important a piece of equipment to a bartender as the shaker was in the 1930s.

AMA

Above
Five Havana bartenders competing in the 1931 annual cocktail-making contest to see who mixed the meanest.

VINO
VERMOUTH
CONFEZIONATO
PER
ESPORTAZIONE
DELLA
CASA
MARTINI, SOLA E C.
TORINO
STABILIMENTO IN PESSIONE
ARTINI SOLA E C.IA
TORINO
VIA CARLO ALBERTO
STABILIMENTO IN PESSIONE

THE MARTINI

CONSIDER THE DRY MARTINI. JUST ABOUT EVERYONE HAS AN OPINION ON HOW TO MAKE THE PERFECT MARTINI. EVERY BARTENDER BELIEVES HIS MAGIC COMBINATION OF GIN AND VERMOUTH WILL PRODUCE A STATE OF MIND SOMEWHERE BETWEEN HAPPINESS AND SHEER ECSTASY. THEY ARE RIGHT.

Throughout its history, the Martini has been, and still is, the drink of the rich and famous – everyone from John D. Rockefeller and Noel Coward to Harrison Ford. It is the drink people aspire to, and has perhaps been the cause of more marriages, arguments and divorces than any other alcoholic combination. It is also responsible for that 1950s and 60s American phenomenon, the three-Martini lunch.

Opposite
A collection of early 19th-century Turin vermouth bottles.

There are many, many myths surrounding the creation of the Martini – if God created Man, then who on earth created the Martini? Some believe it was the legendary bartender "Professor" Jerry Thomas. Thomas had arrived in San Francisco during the Gold Rush and worked at the El Dorado as a bartender. Later,

The Dave Brubeck Quartet's alto sax player Paul Desmond said in an interview that he aimed to "sound like a dry Martini".

he moved to the Occidental Hotel and this is where the Martini myth was created. A man on his way to the town of Martinez walked in, placed a gold nugget on the bar, and asked Thomas to make him a drink to remember. In his book, *The Martini*, Barnaby Conrad III quotes: "Very well, here is a new drink I have invented for your trip," said Thomas. "We'll call it the Martinez." There is no date recorded for this exchange, but a 1927 interview with the bartender mentions the tale.

In the 1887 edition of Thomas' book, *The Bar-Tender's Guide*, one of the 24 recipes was the Martinez. This recipe required "one dash of bitters, two dashes of maraschino, one glass of vermouth, two small lumps of ice and a pony of Old Tom gin. The bartender was instructed to shake this mixture and strain it into a cocktail glass and garnish with a slice of lemon.

This is not the drink we have come to know as the Martini.

By the early 1900s, many publishers were printing bartenders' guides – and including a recipe for a drink called The Martini, made of sweet vermouth and gin in equal quantities, with a dash of orange bitters as an optional finish to the recipe.

As its popularity grew, more people laid claim to its creation, including the small town of Martinez, California. The town claims that in

1870 a miner from San Francisco stopped at Richelieu's salon in Martinez to refill a bottle of whiskey. The bartender filled the container, but the miner was not satisfied, so Richelieu mixed him a small drink, dropped an olive into it and told the miner this was a Martinez cocktail. Richelieu left Martinez to run salons in San Francisco, and it is well documented that the Martinez was his speciality during the 1880s. Although there is no verified and published recipe, the town of Martinez still firmly claims that it is the birthplace of the Martini and in 1992 a group of citizens erected a brass plaque to that effect.

Another legend involves an immigrant bartender, Martini di Arma di Taggia. His turf was New York's Knickerbocker Hotel where he claimed he had mixed a drink of dry gin, dry vermouth and orange bitters. This story was reinforced by author John Doxat who spoke to another Italian bartender – Luigi of the Savoia Majestic Hotel in Genoa. Luigi remembered drinking di Taggia's Martini at The Knickerbocker Hotel in 1912 – but this is still a bit later than Thomas'.

The English, too, have created a legend around the origin of the name. The name comes from, they say, the Martini & Henry rifle (invented by Friedrich von Martini) and used by the British Army between 1871 and 1891.

"A well-made Martini or Gibson, correctly chilled and nicely served, has been more often my true friend than any other two-legged creature."
M.F.K. FISHER, 1949

Above
In the spotlight – the bar as stage at the Grand Hotel, Torquay, in 1951.

The *Oxford English Dictionary* states the earliest use of the word Martini was in 1894, in an advertisement for Heublein's Club Cocktails, a range of pre-mixed cocktails. Unfortunately, the *OED* incorrectly states that Martini originates from the vermouth brand of Martini & Rossi but the brand was not imported into the United States at that time.

An early edition of bartender Thomas Stuart's *Fancy Drinks and How To Mix Them*, published in 1896, featured a recipe that very much resembles what we know as the modern Martini: 1 dash of orange bitters, 2/3 Plymouth gin and 1/3 French vermouth. The gin and the vermouth were both dry in taste, and the orange bitters has been an ingredient of the Martini up until the 1950s.

Yet another Martinez recipe appeared in the 1884 edition of *The Modern Bartender's Guide*

– three years before Jerry Thomas' publication. Another legendary bartender, Harry Johnson, made the first mention of the word Martini in his *New and Improved Illustrated Bartender's Manual*, published in 1888. This recipe used sweet gin and the illustration is (incorrectly) labelled "martine".

As you can see, it is nigh impossible to decide just who did invent the drink we know today as the Martini. What is certain is that by 1900 the word was familiar to bartenders in the United States and in Europe. The drink was also on everyone's lips.

By the First World War, the Martini was the most popular American cocktail. Its fame crossed the Atlantic and soon Europeans were indulging in the alluring drink. In 1917 the tabloid New York Sun ran a spoof anthropological story on Dri Mart Ini, an ancient Egyptian god of thirst, priest of the goddess Isis. The god was allegedly "shaking a drink in a covered urn of glass while the 15th pharaoh of the dynasty Lush is shown with a protruding tongue quivering with expectation".

Actress Clara Bow referred to the Martini as "a longer word for joy".

When Prohibition was declared on 17 January, 1920, the selling of alcohol was prohibited. Gin became the bootlegger's currency – as it was easier to make than whiskey. The gin aged in the time it took to travel from the bathroom to wherever the party

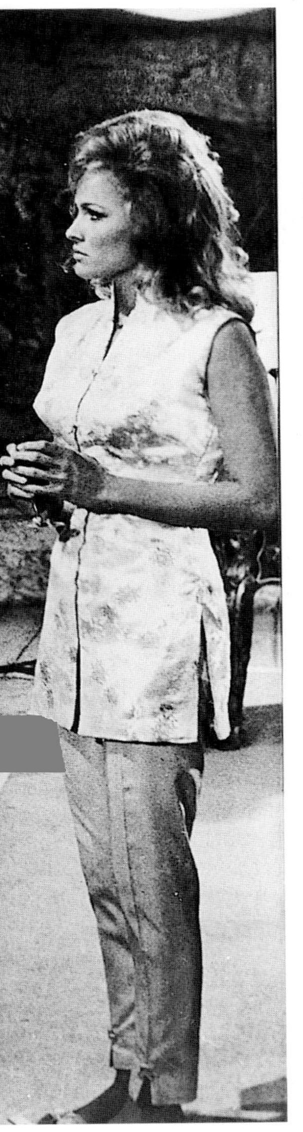

Left
Double agent – the ultra-suave James Bond (pictured here played by Sean Connery in Dr No) was probably the Martini's greatest ambassador during the Cold War era. But he must also shoulder the blame for perpetuating the myth that a Martini should be shaken and not stirred.

Opposite
A sedate-looking Martini party 60s-style. The rather more outrageous Dorothy Parker claimed, "after three I'm under the table. After four I'm under the host".

was in progress. To disguise the taste of bathtub gin, a measure of vermouth in a one-to-two ratio was added. The cocktail was sipped from a small chilled glass with a twist of lemon; the latter also helping to disguise the rather disgusting taste of the gin.

Gradually, the amount of gin in the vermouth became larger – by the 40s, the ratio was 3–4 parts gin and 1 part vermouth. The more gin, the drier the Martini.

THE DREAM MAKER

The Martini became the symbol of the American Dream and, when President Franklin D. Roosevelt mixed the first legal Martini in the White House when Prohibition ended in December 1933, he gave the cocktail an unofficial status. The subliminal message: "Drink Martinis and you, too, could become President of the United States."

Roosevelt also used the Martini as a bargaining tool – he served the Russian leader Stalin with a Martini during the 1943 Teheran Conference. Stalin remarked the drink was cold to his stomach. A Roosevelt aide described these years as "the four martinis and let's have an agreement" era. The Martini cocktail was later regarded by the Russian leader, Kruschev, as America's lethal weapon. The former US Secretary of State Dean Acheson knew of its seductive abilities. Richard Nixon liked his

Time of your life!
Martini belongs to life's best moments. It is, after all, made by perfectionists in taste. Chilled? With soda? "On the rocks"? Take your choice. Then take your time, and let Martini itself reveal the delightful secret of its international fame.
MARTINI
Vermouth
Time for Martini on the rocks!
MARTINI
MARTINI
In the U.S. it's MARTINI & ROSSI, in the rest of the world it's simply Martini, wherever you go it's the same superb vermouth.

Martinis at a ratio of seven-to-one. Former American president Gerald Ford was known to drink the occasional Martini until his doctor recommended he give them up.

Martinis & the Imagination

Not only the politically powerful imbibed: Hollywood adopted the Martini as the socially acceptable screen cocktail. Off screen, its producers, writers and performers regularly sipped the lethal liquid combination. Character actor Charles Butterworth has been credited

with delivering the line: "I must get out of these wet clothes and into a dry Martini." in 1937.

Movie celebrities such as Humphrey Bogart, William Holden and W. C. Fields (who had them for breakfast) were also admirers of the pleasures of this diamond-clear cocktail.

American writer Ernest Hemingway and his characters drank Martinis; English writer Somerset Maugham wrote that the Martini should be stirred not shaken, so that the molecules lie sensuously on top of each other. (He used gin and Noilly Prat vermouth). James Bond, being a rebel by nature, drank Martinis "shaken not stirred". His creator, Ian Fleming, altered the traditional gin base to vodka and in *Casino Royale* had Bond mix a Vesper (in memory of double agent Vesper Lynd) – three parts gin, one part vodka and a dash of Kina Lilet (a golden French vermouth). It was shaken and served with a slice of lemon peel.

Opposite
W. C. Fields kept a cold flask of Martini stashed on the set of his films, referring to it as his "pineapple juice".

DRY OR DRIER?

The dryness of the Martini became a talking point throughout the next decade. Hard-core Martini drinkers thought that a coating of vermouth on the mixing glass was, indeed, more than enough. Originally, in the 1900s, the Martini was created using the combination of one part gin to one part vermouth, but then another version of the same period was two parts gin to one part vermouth, which is

Sir Winston Churchill would make his Martinis by pouring gin into a pitcher and "glancing briefly at a bottle of vermouth" across the room. He preferred the gin made for his club, Boodles.

perhaps where the dryness came in the title – dry Martini.

Yet by the early 1940s, the Martini had become even drier and some of the recipes had four parts of gin and one part vermouth (still in the same size glass) but then by the early 70s it had developed into nine parts gin to one part vermouth. Now, the ratio is closer to a naked Martini – that means, only a whiff of vermouth.

But the real task was to make the Martini as cold as possible. Deep frozen ice cubes and frozen glasses seem to have been the best way of achieving this. Even now, erudite discussions on how dry a Martini should be are conducted by the sanest of men and women.

Remains a Classic

Opposite *The Martini has always been a stylish accessory among the fast set. The finishing touch to the latest fashionable ensemble.*

By 1968 the power of the Martini was at its zenith, but breathalysers and an ailing economy required the American working man to wean himself from the liquid lunch. In 1978, a New York newspaper columnist wrote that he feared the Martini would become extinct. During the 80s and early 90s the Martini remained deep in the memory of the connoisseur.

Recent years have seen the Martini in a surprise comeback – but this generation's taste buds have moved on from gin to vodka. A

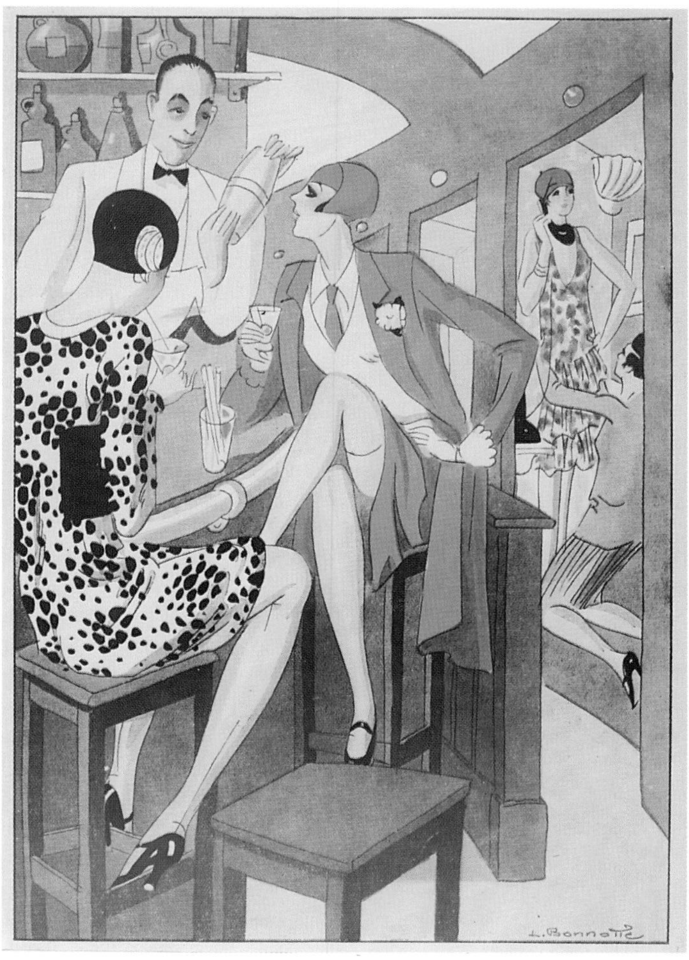

Opposite *Actress Zsa Zsa Gabor – as fussy about her vodka as her husbands – advertises Smirnoff in the 1960s.*

recipe for a vodkatini appeared in *Bottoms Up* by Ted Saucier back in 1951. The combination was provided by a society photographer, Jerome Zerbe. That was 45 years ago, when vodka was a spirit new to the American palate.

Certainly the marketing by companies such as Smirnoff in the 1960s featuring, amongst others, a female cosmonaut, actor and film director Woody Allen, comedian Harpo Marx and jazz clarinet giant Benny Goodman, rivalled the imagination and subtlety of the earlier gin advertisements. It is also entirely possible that James Bond's vodkatini had much do with the drink's surge in popularity.

A vodka Martini is now the most requested mixed cocktail in power-broking territory – Washington, DC – and throughout Europe and America the Martini, made with gin or vodka, is enjoying a resurgence. Vodka has introduced the Martini to the young who, many social observers feel, are tired of asking for a glass of white wine, or a beer, and want something with a bit more oomph. The vodkatini promises to provide.

Here are three versions of the classic dry Martini. There are also two other recipes – one uses sweet vermouth and is known as the Sweet Martini or Gin and It; the other is the Perfect Martini, a mixture of sweet vermouth and dry vermouth (in equal proportions) and of gin.

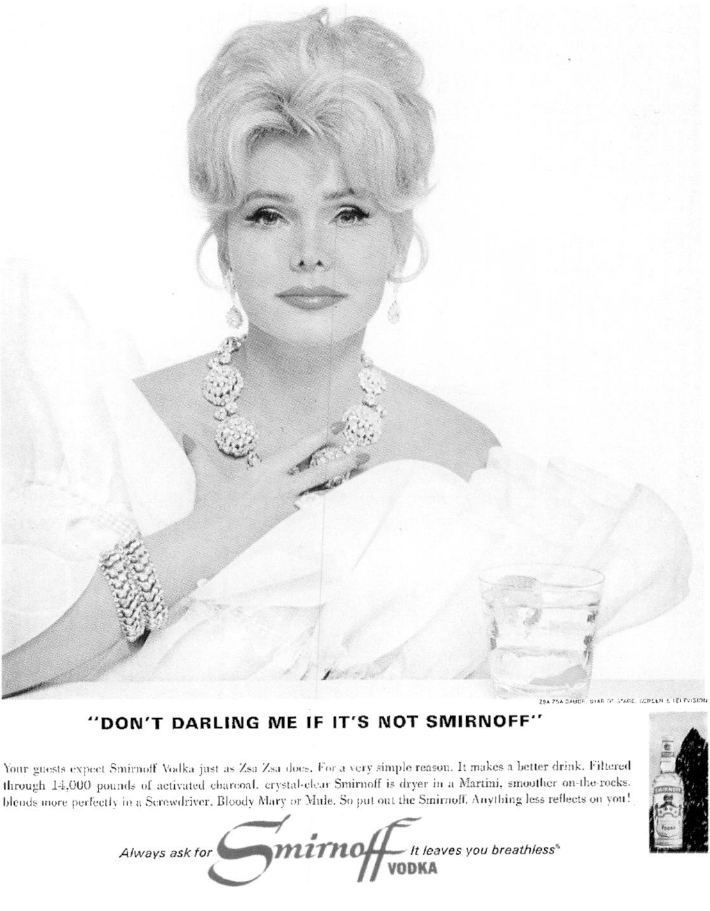

ZSA ZSA GABOR, STAR OF STAGE, SCREEN & TELEVISION

"DON'T DARLING ME IF IT'S NOT SMIRNOFF"

Your guests expect Smirnoff Vodka just as Zsa Zsa does. For a very simple reason. It makes a better drink. Filtered through 14,000 pounds of activated charcoal, crystal-clear Smirnoff is dryer in a Martini, smoother on-the-rocks, blends more perfectly in a Screwdriver, Bloody Mary or Mule. So put out the Smirnoff. Anything less reflects on you!

MY DRY MARTINI

Kingsley Amis, writing in the *Illustrated London News*, said of my Martini: "We all know...how difficult it is to produce not just a well-balanced Dry Martini but simply one that stays cold enough without the base recourse to ice-cubes in the drink. It was achieved all right."

METHOD : direct
GLASS : cocktail

8cl/2 3/4oz gin
1-2 drops Martini Extra Dry vermouth

Put a bottle of excellent gin (or vodka) in the freezer. Put the glass in freezer. This will help you to be quicker when you serve the drink. Put the vermouth into an old Angostura bottle with a pourer that produces a drop.

I do not mix the Martini – I pour it straight into the glass and, over the top, I lay just two to three drops of vermouth. This gives a little nose of the vermouth.

Cut a twist of lemon – try to cut it as thin as possible – then face the twist upside-down to the glass and twist it to give a few tears of the lemon to the glass. Run the lemon twist around the rim of the glass and then you have the perfect Martini. Olive is optional.

"When coming to London, first have Salvatore make you a Martini. Salvatore makes the best Martini in England."
STANTON DELAPLANE, SAN FRANCISCO CHRONICLE, MARTINI-LOVER.

Opposite
Dry Martini.

GIBSON

METHOD : stir
GLASS: cocktail

8cl/2 3/4oz gin
a drop of dry vermouth
1 white pearl onion

There are a few myths surrounding this cocktail but it seems most likely it was invented in the 1940s for American artist Charles Dana Gibson at The Player's Club, New York. As there were no olives, he used a white pearl onion.

Pour the gin into a mixing glass with ice. Add the dry vermouth and stir in a clockwise direction. Add the pearl onion and serve.

VODKATINI

METHOD : stir
GLASS : cocktail

8cl/2 3/4oz vodka
1-2 dashes vermouth

Before James Bond asked for his Martini shaken not stirred, the Martini was gin-based. The vodkatini is now as popular as the gin dry Martini, but most bartenders would refuse to shake a Martini. Including me!

Pour the vodka into the glass with ice, add the vermouth. Stir quickly and serve with an olive or a twist as requested.

Opposite
A Martini-drinker's idea of heaven in a glass.

..du soleil dans un verre..
COGNAC
MONNET

THE REST

CLASSIC COCKTAIL RECIPES HAVE NOT CHANGED MUCH. YET THERE ARE INSTANCES WHERE THE ORIGINAL RECIPE HAS BEEN ALTERED. WHENEVER THIS HAS HAPPENED, AN EXPLANATION (IF IT EXISTS!) IS GIVEN. WHERE THE STORY (OR MYTH) OF A COCKTAIL'S CREATION IS KNOWN, IT IS ALSO GIVEN.

Styles and sizes of glasses vary from country to country and from bar to bar. The following sizes are a guide for the recipes in this book.

champagne flute: 20cl/7½oz
cocktail: 11cl/4oz
goblet: 35cl/12oz
highball: 35cl/12oz
old-fashioned: 30cl/10oz
pilsener: 35cl/12oz
piña colada: 40cl/14oz
shot: 5.7cl/2oz

To avoid repeating the instructions for ice throughout the book, I've made the following simple rules:

Method: **shaker** or **mixing glass** – it is assumed that the method container is always filled with ice.

Opposite
A kiss on the lip – the analogy of the cocktail as a sexual aperitif is deeply ingrained in all its iconography.

Method: **build** – the drink is always built on ice in the glass unless otherwise stated.

Glass: drinks served in a **cocktail glass** or **champagne flute** never have ice in the glass whatever the method.

Any exceptions to these rules are clearly stated in the method.

The recipes are my choice of classic cocktails – others are welcome to dispute them over a dry Martini in my bar.

ADONIS

METHOD : mixing glass
GLASS : cocktail

5cl/1¾oz dry sherry
3cl/1oz sweet vermouth
dash orange bitters

An aperitif, it was first mixed in 1886 to celebrate the success of a Broadway musical. There is no mention of either the male lead or the barman looking like a Greek Adonis, so the legacy of the name itself remains a mystery. The drink remained popular until the 1950s and 60s when the long drink became more fashionable.

Pour the dry sherry into a mixing glass, add the vermouth, stir and strain into the glass. Add a dash of orange bitters. To garnish, add a twist of orange peel.

AFFINITY

Once fashionable in the 1920s, this classic aperitif is one for the purist.

Pour both vermouths into the mixing glass, add the whisky and a dash of Angostura. Stir and strain into a cocktail glass. A final touch: squeeze a twist of lemon over the drink, but do not add it to the drink.

METHOD : mixing glass
GLASS : cocktail

3cl/1oz Scotch whisky
3cl/1oz sweet vermouth
3cl/1oz dry vermouth
dash Angostura bitters

ALFONSO

A champagne cocktail named after the deposed Spanish King Alfonso XIII (1886-1941), who first had the pleasure of tasting this combination while in exile in France.

Place the cube of sugar in a chilled champagne flute and soak with the Angostura. Add the Dubonnet and finish with champagne and stir. Squeeze the twist of lemon on top of the drink, but do not add.

METHOD : build
GLASS : flute

3cl/1oz Dubonnet
1 sugar cube
2 dashes Angostura bitters
champagne

Americano

Method : build
Glass : highball

3.75cl/1 1/3oz Campari
3.75cl/1 1/3oz sweet vermouth
soda water

An aperitif to stimulate the palate, this is the forebearer of the Negroni (see page 145) without the juniper flavour of the gin.

Pour the sweet vermouth, then the Campari into the glass. Garnish with lemon and orange twists. Soda water (club soda) is optional – the soda water gives the drink its freshness.

Angel's Tit

Method : build (no ice)
Glass : cocktail

4cl/1 1/2oz Maraschino
2cl/2/3oz fresh cream

This was one of the most popular Prohibition after-dinner drinks. The name makes perfect sense once you see and then taste this divine cocktail.

Pour the Maraschino in first, add the cream. Garnish with a red Maraschino cherry in the centre of the creamy top.

Opposite
A Prohibition angel makes a seductive case for the cocktail hour.

LEO FONTAN

Bacardi Classic

Only Bacardi white rum can be used to make this drink. In September 1936 a temporary injunction to restrain the Barbizon-Plaza Hotel and the Winel Restaurant in New York from selling Bacardi cocktails unless they contained Bacardi rum was denied. The company won a permanent injunction when the case went to trial at the New York Supreme Court later that year.

Pour the ingredients into a shaker. Shake well and strain into the glass. Garnish with a cherry on a stick across the rim of the glass.

Method : shake
Glass : cocktail

5cl/1 3/4oz Bacardi white rum
3cl/1oz fresh lime juice
1 teaspoon Grenadine

Opposite
Old-Fashioned (left) and Bacardi Classic (right).

B-52

Pour the Kahlua into the glass first. Over the back of a bar spoon, gently pour the Bailey's and then pour the Grand Marnier over the back of the bar spoon to finish the drink. Serve with a stirrer on the side. This will give you a colourful three-layered drink and you can sip each layer for its flavour, or stir it. ***Page 171.***

Method : build (no ice)
Glass : shot or sherry/port

2cl/2/3oz Kahlua
2cl/2/3oz Bailey's Irish Cream
2cl/2/3oz Grand Marnier

Bellini

Method : build
Glass : flute

fresh peach juice
dry sparkling wine (methode champenoise) or champagne

In 1943 an exhibition of work by Venetian painter Bellini inspired Giuseppi Cipriani, the bartender at Harry's Bar in Venice, to create this extraordinarily famous champagne and peach juice cocktail. It was a favourite of Ernest Hemingway and Noel Coward when they were in town.

Always use fresh white peach juice purée. When the peach is in season, blanch to remove the skins, remove stone, place in a blender with a touch of fresh lemon juice, blend for a few seconds and then freeze ready for the summer.

A bellini not made with fresh peach juice is not a bellini!

Opposite
Golden Cadillac (centre) Sea Breeze (left) and Bellini (right).

Quarter-fill a chilled flute with peach juice and finish with the sparkling wine/champagne and stir. Garnish with a wedge of peach on the rim of the glass.

Between the Sheets

Method : shake
Glass : cocktail

dash fresh lemon juice
3cl/1oz brandy
3cl/1oz Cointreau
3cl/1oz Bacardi rum

Created in the 1930s, the name of this cocktail is the ultimate double entendre. Does the drink's name intimate seduction, or is there another hidden meaning? The general vote is for seduction, since it is an after-dinner drink. This combination is definitely very seductive.

Pour the lemon juice, brandy, rum and Cointreau into a shaker, shake sharply and strain into the glass.

Black Russian

Method : build
Glass : old-fashioned

4cl/1 1/2oz vodka
2cl/2/3oz Kahlua

A short after-dinner drink, it is vodka with a dark finish. Although it reached the height of its popularity in the 1950s, it is still popular.

Build into an old-fashioned glass, pouring the vodka first, then the Kahlua and stir. Serve with a stirrer.

BLACK VELVET

Traditionally, this was served in a beer tankard but its container these days is usually a champagne flute. A simple, velvet-smooth champagne cocktail, it was created by the bartender at Brooks' Club, London, in 1861. England was in mourning for Prince Albert and he felt that the champagne also ought to be in mourning and combined it with the dark Guinness. The mixture was also the favourite tipple of Prince Otto Von Bismarck of Germany.

METHOD : build (no ice)
GLASS : beer/flute

draught or bottled Guinness
champagne

Half-fill the glass with Guinness and gently finish with champagne. ***Page 131.***

BLOODY CAESAR

METHOD : build/shake
GLASS : highball

5cl/1 3/4oz vodka
15cl/5 1/2oz clamato juice (mixture of tomato and clam juice)
2cl/2/3oz fresh lemon juice
pinch of celery salt
dash Tabasco sauce
2 dashes Worcestershire sauce
black pepper

This invigorating and restorative long drink was created for crooner Tony Bennett while he was performing in Las Vegas. On a night when he'd had one too many to drink and needed a quick reviver, a barman at the Caeser's Palace hotel fixed him up this concoction.

To build: pour the clamato and lemon juices over ice in a highball glass; add the vodka. Add spices and stir. To shake: use the same method in a shaker and shake sharply. Strain into a highball glass. Add a quick twist of ground black pepper. Garnish with a wedge of lime sitting on the rim of the glass and add a cocktail stirrer.

BLOODY MARY

METHOD : build/shake
GLASS : highball

5cl/1 3/4oz vodka
15cl/5 1/2oz tomato juice
2 dashes Worcestershire sauce
2cl/2/3oz fresh lemon juice
pinch of celery salt
1-2 dashes of Tabasco sauce
black pepper

Harry's New York Bar, Paris, was the birthplace of this classic restorative cocktail. The year was 1921. Fernand "Pete" Petiot combined tomato juice, vodka, salt, pepper and Worcestershire sauce. There was nothing new about the vodka and tomato juice combination, but there was something new about the spice and the name – his inspiration was the Hollywood actress Mary Pickford (who has a cocktail of rum, Grenadine and Maraschino, named after her).

In 1934, a year after Prohibition had ended in America, Petiot accepted an invitation from John Astor of the St Regis Hotel, New York, to become its head bartender. As the name may have been offensive to some people, the drink was launched there under the name Red Snapper, which did not have the same ring to it. A customer, Prince Serge Obolensky, requested the drink be "spiced up". The Tabasco sauce was added and it was a hit with everybody's palate. The recipe was then circulated amongst bartenders under its original name, Bloody Mary.

The origins of the celery stick garnish date back to the 1960s and are attributed to the inventiveness of a guest at The Pump Room in the Ambassador East Hotel, Chicago. The guest was served a Bloody Mary without the customary swizzle stick, so she picked a celery stick from a nearby garnish tray and used this to stir the drink. The maitre d' noticed, and hence the celery stick garnish was born. Should one eat it? Yes, if you are hungry. Otherwise, stir and put to one side. Many bartenders prefer not to add the celery stick.

To build: pour the tomato and lemon juices over the ice in the glass; add the vodka. Add spices and stir. To shake: use the same method in a shaker and shake sharply. Strain into a highball glass. Add a quick twist of ground black pepper. Garnish with a wedge of lime sitting on the rim of the glass and add the celery stick (if preferred) and a stirrer.

Making a Bloody Mary is like cooking a very fine steak. Always ask how the guest prefers the drink – at its best, it is a long, cool and refreshing drink. I prefer to use a combination of lime and lemon juice to give a less sharp finish to the drink. Many bartenders add non-traditional ingredients such as horseradish sauce and mustard, but it is important to retain the original characteristic of the recipe.

Opposite
Moscow Mule (left) and Bloody Mary (right).

BLUE BLAZER

METHOD : Muddle
GLASS : two silver tankards (by no means essential but fun to try)

5cl/1 $^{3}/_{4}$oz whisky
5cl/1 $^{3}/_{4}$oz boiling water
1 bar spoon caster sugar (or clear honey)
juice of half a lemon (originally only lemon peel was used)

Created by the legendary "Professor" Jerry Thomas, while he was in residence at the bar of the El Dorado, San Francisco. Thomas was a star performer and, with this drink, he perfected the technique of igniting the whisky and throwing the flaming liquid between two silver tankards – mixing the ingredients whilst the bar was aflame. This brilliant act impressed President Grant so much that he presented him with a cigar.

Thomas was a man of principle – he refused to serve this drink until the thermometer fell below 10°C (50°F). If you had a cold or a bout of influenza, then he might have made an exception, for the Blue Blazer is reputed to make the symptoms a little more bearable (yet another doctor to the rescue!). So if you are hosting a mid-winter cocktail party or you have a needy customer at the bar and you want to show off your skill, this is the drink to perfect.

Heat the whisky in a small saucepan and pour into one tankard. Put the boiling water into the other tankard. Light the whisky and, while it is flaming, pour the two liquids from one tankard to the other four or five times. This may seem difficult at first and practice is required before you perform this magical act in front of guests. If you want to make a longer stream of flame, the trick is to move the pouring arm in a smooth, upward movement as you pour the liquid into the second, stationary tankard. Sweeten with sugar or honey. Garnish with a twist of lemon.

BLUE LAGOON

Andy MacElhone, the son of Harry of Harry's New York Bar, Paris, created this colourful long drink in the 1960s when blue Curaçao first appeared in a bottle. Andy originally served a Blue Lagoon with fresh lemon juice instead of the lemonade, which is popular now.

METHOD : build
GLASS : highball

3cl/1oz vodka
3cl/1oz blue Curaçao
lemonade

Pour the blue Curaçao and the vodka into the glass. Finish with the lemonade. Garnish with a Maraschino cherry and a slice of lemon.

Bossa Nova

Method : shake
Glass : highball

3cl/1oz Galliano
3cl/1oz white rum
1.5cl/½oz apricot brandy
1.5cl/½oz lemon juice
3cl/1oz pineapple juice
dash egg white

A long drink with all of the excitement of the South American rhythm from which it takes its name. It has a wonderful almond/apricot taste with a sweet and sour finish.

Pour all ingredients into a shaker and shake sharply. Strain into the glass and garnish with a slice of pineapple and a sprig of mint on the rim of the glass. Serve with a straw and a stirrer.

BOSTON FLIP

The flip was traditionally made by the old method of flipping the combination between two containers to obtain a smooth consistency. In the 17th century a flip featured beaten eggs, sugar, spices, rum and a hot ale. The innkeeper would mull the mixture with a hot iron "loggerhead" before serving it. The cocktail has changed dramatically since then. It is now a short drink, served cold with a finish of sprinkled nutmeg. It can be made with any spirit, and egg yolks. Milk is not used in the drink, otherwise it becomes an Egg Nog.

Pour the spirits, gomme syrup and the egg yolk in a shaker. Shake sharply. Strain and pour into the glass. Grate fresh nutmeg across the top of the drink.

Another popular version is the Brandy Flip, which is made exactly as above, but without the Madeira.

METHOD : shake
GLASS : wine glass

3.5cl/1 1/4oz bourbon whiskey
3.5cl/1 1/4oz Madeira
1 egg yolk
dash gomme syrup

Brandy Alexander

Method : shake
Glass : cocktail

3cl/1oz brandy
3cl/1oz dark brown crême de cacao
3cl/1oz fresh cream

A sophisticated after-dinner drink that is very popular with cocktail drinkers. An interesting point: the Alexander was originally a gin-based cocktail.

Pour the crême de cacao and cream into a shaker. Add the brandy. Shake sharply and strain into the glass. To garnish: grate fresh nutmeg over the top of the drink.

Bronx

Method : shake
Glass : cocktail

1.5cl/1/2oz sweet vermouth
1.5cl/1/2oz dry vermouth
3cl/1oz gin
juice of 1/4 orange

A pre-dinner drink inspired by a visit to the Bronx Zoo in 1906 by Johnny Solon, renown bartender at the Waldorf Astoria, New York. Johnny served his drink in a cocktail glass.

Pour the two vermouths and the fresh orange juice into a shaker and add the gin. Shake sharply and strain into the glass. Garnish with a quarter of a slice of orange on the rim of the glass.

Opposite
A 1935 advertisement extolling the virtues of gin.

The Choice
of Connoisseurs
for 130 Years

SEAGER'S
GIN

*The Spirit
of To-day...*

AND TO-MORROW

SEAGER, EVANS & CO., LTD.
LONDON, S.E.8.

Opposite *Napoleon's brandy, hero of the cocktail hour – "Claret is the liquor for boys; port for men; but he who aspires to be a hero must drink brandy." Samuel Johnson.*

IER COGNAC
N'S BRANDY

-LA VEUVE JOYEUSE-

BUCK'S FIZZ

Mr McGarry, bartender at Buck's Club, London, created this combination in 1921, the beginning of the Roaring Twenties. His recipe is very specific about the ratio of 2/3 champagne to 1/3 of fresh orange juice.

Squeeze enough fresh orange juice to fill a quarter of a frosted champagne flute. Fill slowly with champagne and stir.

METHOD : build
GLASS : flute

fresh orange juice
dry champagne

BULLSHOT

It is said that if you don't want to start lunch with soup, then start with a Bullshot – an invigorating drink, full of strong flavour, finishing with the sharpness of lemon.

Pour the beef bouillon, lemon juice, Tabasco and Worcestershire sauce into a shaker, add the vodka and shake sharply. Strain into the glass. Add a quick twist of black pepper. Garnish with a wedge of lime sitting on the rim of the glass. Serve with a stirrer.

METHOD : shake
GLASS : highball

5cl/1 3/4oz vodka
15cl/5 1/2oz beef bouillon
dash fresh lemon juice
2 dashes Worcestershire sauce
celery salt
Tabasco
black pepper to taste

Caipirinha

Method : build
Glass : old-fashioned

5cl/1 3/4oz Aguardente de Cana – cachaça
1 small fresh lime
1 1/2 teaspoons caster sugar

A Brazilian bartender's speciality, its name translates literally as "peasant's drink". Many refer to it as the cocktail to replace the malaria shot.

Wash the lime and remove the top and the bottom and cut into small segments (from top to bottom). Add the sugar and the lime pieces to the glass. Crush the lime to make juice. Muddle to ensure the sugar has dissolved. Add dry ice cubes to fill the glass, add the cachaça and stir. Serve with a stirrer.

Cape Codder

Method : build
Glass : highball

5cl/1 3/4oz vodka
15cl/5 1/2oz cranberry juice

Named after the summer resort on the Massachusetts coast, this refreshing, long drink should be sipped on the porch before lunch or as the sun sets on the horizon.

Pour the cranberry juice over ice in a glass, add the vodka. Stir well. Garnish with a wedge of lime slipped on the edge of the glass. Serve with a stirrer.

Opposite
Margarita (left), Strawberry Daiquiri (centre) and Caipirinha (right).

Classic Champagne Cocktail

Method : build
Glass : flute

champagne
2cl/$\frac{2}{3}$oz cognac
2 dashes Angostura bitters
1 sugar cube

The origin of this recipe is shrouded in mystery but its journey into cocktail history is interesting. In 1889, a New York journalist organised a competition among New York bartenders. Their mission: to create a new cocktail. The prize: a gold medal. A Mr John Dougherty won with a drink he called Business Brace, saying that he had discovered the recipe 25 years previously in the southern states. The original recipe included a small amount of spring water.

Place the sugar cube in the champagne flute and soak with the Angostura. Add the cognac and finish with the champagne. Garnish with a slice of orange and a red Maraschino cherry.

There are many stories surrounding champagne. An early tale describes an encounter between Napoleon Bonaparte and Monsieur Jean-Remy Moët shortly before a battle in the dawn hours of 18th March 1814.

"If I should fail, within a month I shall be either dead or dethroned. So I want to reward you now for the admirable way you have built up your business and all you have done for our wines abroad."

NAPOLEON THEN TOOK OFF HIS CHEVALIER'S CROSS OF THE LEGION OF HONOUR AND PINNED IT ON M. JEAN-REMY MOËT'S CHEST.

Corpse Reviver

No 1
Method : stir
Glass : cocktail

3cl/1oz brandy
2cl/2/3oz sweet vermouth
2cl/2/3oz Calvados

No 2
Method : shake
Glass : cocktail

1.5cl/1/2oz lemon juice
1.5cl/1/2oz Lillet
1.5cl/1/2oz Cointreau
1.5cl/1/2oz gin
1 dash absinthe (Pernod)

No 3
Method : stir
Glass : cocktail

3cl/1oz brandy
3cl/1oz crême de menthe (white)
3cl/1oz Fernet-Branca

Created by Frank Meier at the Ritz Bar, Paris, in the 1920s and immortalised in *The Savoy Cocktail Book* with: "To be taken before 11am, or whenever steam and energy are needed."

Harry Craddock added that "four of Corpse Reviver No. 2 taken in quick succession will unrevive the corpse!" Corpse Reviver No. 3 was created by Johnny Johnson of the Savoy circa 1948 and is still a popular revival cocktail at the Savoy's American Bar.

No 1

Pour the brandy, Calvados and sweet vermouth into a mixing glass. Stir and strain into a glass. Harry Craddock liked to shake the mixture but I stir it.

No. 2

Put all ingredients in a shaker and shake sharply. Strain into a cocktail glass.

No.3

Pour the ingredients into a mixing glass, stir and strain into a cocktail glass.

COSMOPOLITAN

A relatively new drink created in America, this Martini-style aperitif has become popular and I predict it will be a classic.

Pour ingredients into the shaker and shake sharply. Strain into the glass. Garnish with a twist of lime. ***Page 160.***

METHOD : shake
GLASS : cocktail

5cl/1 3/4oz vodka
1cl/1/3oz Cointreau
1cl/1/3oz cranberry juice
1cl/1/3oz fresh lime juice

CUBA LIBRE

One of the best-known rum drinks in the world, the Cuba Libre is attributed to an army lieutenant in Cuba mixing Barcardi rum with a new soft drink called Coca Cola – this was in 1893.

Pour the juice then the rum into the glass. Finish with the Coca Cola. Garnish with a wedge of lime sitting on the rim of the glass. Serve with a stirrer.

METHOD : build
GLASS : highball

5cl/1 3/4oz Bacardi white rum
juice of 1 fresh lime
Coca Cola

DAIQUIRI

METHOD : shake
GLASS : cocktail

5cl/1¾oz white rum
3cl/1oz fresh lime juice
2-3 dashes gomme syrup

Ernest Hemingway's nickname at La Floradita Bar, Havana was Papa Dobles as the writer always ordered double daiquiris.

Marlene Dietrich was often seen lounging on a sofa in the Savoy's American Bar with a daiquiri in her hand.

Opposite
Pina Colada (left), Hurricane Marilyn (centre) and classic Daiquiri (right).

The original daiquiri – a combination of rum, lime and sugar – was created by Jennings Cox, an American mining engineer working in Cuba. He worked for the Pennsylvania Steel Company and Cuba's Spanish-American Iron Company. In the long, hot summer of 1896 his supplies of gin ran out – and he was expecting some VIPs for drinks. The only liquor available was rum and he did not want to serve straight rum, so he mixed fresh lime juice and granulated sugar to add to the rum.

The drink was named after Daiquiri, a town near Santiago. Its fame spread to America in 1909 when Admiral Lucius Johnson of the US Navy brought the drink back to the United States and Washington's Army and Navy Club. There is a brass plaque dedicated to Cox in its Daiquiri lounge.

Pour all the ingredients into a shaker. Shake sharply. Strain into a cocktail glass. Garnish with a wedge of lime on the rim of the glass.

DUBONNET COCKTAIL

METHOD : mixing glass
GLASS : cocktail

4cl/1 1/2oz Dubonnet
4cl/1 1/2oz gin

This truly is a classic pre-dinner cocktail. At the height of its popularity during the late 1920s, it has survived because of its wonderful flavour and colour when combined. Dubonnet, an aromatic wine, brings out the delicate flavour of the juniper berry in the gin.

Pour both ingredients into a mixing glass. Stir and strain into the glass. Garnish with a twist of lemon.

EGG NOG

The traditional Christmas morning drink. Its origins are unclear but the name could date from the 17th-century English habit of adding a beaten egg to a "noggin" – a small mug of strong beer. You can thicken the mixture by adding more egg yolk, or thin it by adding milk. The consistency is a matter of personal taste.

METHOD : shake
GLASS : highball

- **1 fresh egg (preferably free-range)**
- **1 dash of gomme syrup**
- **3cl/1oz brandy**
- **3cl/1oz dark rum**
- **15cl/5½oz milk**
- **nutmeg**

Put all ingredients (except the milk) in a shaker and shake sharply. Strain into a highball glass. Add the milk and stir, then sprinkle fresh grated nutmeg.

This is how the drink is usually served. If you use hot milk, the drink becomes a Hot Egg Nog.

BREAKFAST EGG NOG

Prepare as above and enjoy.

- **1 fresh egg (preferably free-range)**
- **3cl/1oz orange Curaçao**
- **3cl/1oz brandy**
- **15cl/5½oz milk**

El Burro

Method : blender
Glass : piña colada or large goblet

2cl/2/3oz Kahlua
3cl/1oz dark rum
3cl/1oz coconut cream
3cl/1oz fresh cream
half of a banana
crushed ice

A rich, creamy exotic drink with a hint of coffee finish – the rum is responsible for the spicy kick.

Pour all ingredients into the blender (without ice) and whiz for 10 seconds on high. Then add the crushed ice and whiz for 5 seconds on medium. Pour into the glass and garnish with a slice of banana and a sprig of mint.

Fluffy Duck

Method : build
Glass : highball

3cl/1oz Bacardi
3cl/1oz Advocaat
1cl/1/3oz fresh cream
lemonade

Pour the Bacardi and Advocaat into the glass and add the lemonade and mix well. Pour the cream over the back of a spoon so it floats on top of the mixture. Garnish with a strawberry and a sprig of mint in its centre. Serve with a straw and a stirrer.

Left
The lure of champagne is too much for most.

FRENCH 75

A French creation from the imagination of one Henry of Henry's Bar, Paris, to celebrate the fire power of the famous French 75 light field gun, used during the First World War. Originally called the "75 Cocktail", the combination was added to by Harry of Harry's New York Bar, Paris, after the War and became known as the French 75. He added champagne to a short drink with a gin base and a dash of lemon juice.

Pour the fresh lemon juice, gomme syrup and gin into a shaker. Shake well. Strain into the glass. Fill with champagne. Stir.

METHOD : shake
GLASS : flute

2cl/2/3oz gin
juice of half a lemon
2 dashes gomme syrup
champagne

"The moment had arrived for a daiquiri. It was a delicate compound; it elevated my contentment to an even higher pitch. Unquestionably the cocktail on my table was a dangerous agent, for it held in its shallow glass bowl slightly encrusted with undissolved sugar the power of a contemptuous indifference to fate; it set the mind free of responsibility; obliterating both memory and tomorrow, it gave the heart an adventitious feeling of superiority and momentarily vanquished all the celebrated, the eternal fears."

San Cristobal de la Habana by Joseph Hergesheimer

Frozen Daiquiri

Constantino "Constante" Ribailagua of La Floridita Bar in Havana, Cuba, created the first frozen daiquiri in 1912. Not only did he serve it with crushed ice, but he squeezed the lime juice by hand directly into the cocktail shaker. This action releases the lime oil that gives the drink its nose.

The original frozen daiquiri was made in the same way as a daiquiri, only the ingredients were placed in a glass with crushed ice, which has an instant freezing effect. The crushed ice is reponsible for giving the resulting drink the consistency of a light sorbet.

These days its popularity owes much to the invention of the blender. Fresh fruit can be pulverised quickly at the bar, turning the daiquiri into a long drink.

The most popular frozen daiquiri requested today is the Banana Daiquiri, followed closely by Strawberry. You can use any fruit you like – the more imaginative the better. Try not to mix too many flavours together as they will only confuse the palate.

BANANA DAIQUIRI

Pour all the ingredients, including the banana, into the blender. Blend for about 10 seconds then add crushed ice and blend for a few more seconds. This ensures the mixture is not full of melted ice...rather, it instantly freezes the mixture to the correct consistency. Garnish with a slice of kiwi fruit on the rim of the glass. Although the original garnish is a slice of banana, I prefer to use the kiwi because it adds a second colour. Serve with a straw.

METHOD : blender
GLASS : large goblet

4cl/1 1/2oz white rum
2cl/2/3oz crême de banane
2cl/2/3oz fresh lime juice
half of a medium-sized banana

STRAWBERRY DAIQUIRI

Prepare as above. Garnish with a single strawberry and a sprig of mint on the rim of the glass. ***Page 99.***

4cl/1 1/2oz white rum
2cl/2/3oz fraise liqueur
2cl/2/3oz fresh lime juice
4 fresh strawberries

Fuzzy Navel

Method : shake
Glass : highball

3cl/1oz vodka
3cl/1oz peach schnapps
15cl/5½oz orange juice

Pour ingredients into a shaker and shake sharply. Strain into the glass and garnish with a slice of orange and a red Maraschino cherry. Serve with a straw and a stirrer.

Gimlet

Method : build
Glass : old-fashioned

5cl/1¾oz Plymouth gin
2cl/⅔oz Rose's Lime Cordial

When beers and spirits were stored in barrels, bar managers used a small, sharp hand tool, called a gimlet, to tap into them, which has given its name to this small, sharp-tasting cocktail.

Originally made with Plymouth gin – a more assertive and earthy style than London gin, that by law can still only be produced in Plymouth, Devon – the first recipe for this pre-dinner drink was published around 1930. The vodka-based gimlet has now become more common. Rose's is the correct accompaniment whatever the base.

Pour ingredients into a glass filled with ice. Stir, then garnish with a wedge of lime in the drink. Add a stirrer and serve.

Opposite
Gimlet (left) and Manhattan (right).

Discriminating people automatically accept some few names as standards of excellence. In gin, DIXIE BELLE enjoys the enviable favor of those whose taste is unquestioned. Flawless smoothness. Restrained but definite bouquet. Flavor that blends gracefully without overplaying its part. Such superior qualities are the result of surpassing equipment and scientifically controlled distillation in America's Largest Distillery. DIXIE BELLE'S merit, not its moderate price, won overwhelming preference this first year of Repeal. Distilled and bottled by Continental Distilling Corporation, Philadelphia. Another Continental quality liquor is Rittenhouse Square 100 proof Straight Rye Whisky.
Cocktail hour at the Waldorf
In The Oasis Room
DIXIE BELLE
DIXIE BELLE distilled dry GIN

GIN & IT

A perennially favourite lady's drink sipped at around 5pm.

Pour the gin and the vermouth into the chilled glass. Garnish with a red Maraschino cherry and a twist of orange.

METHOD : build
GLASS : old-fashioned

3.5cl/1 1/4oz gin
3.5cl/1 1/4oz sweet vermouth

GIN FIZZ

A long drink that was first mentioned in magazine articles published in the 1870s, the Fizz is a close cousin to the Collins – the difference is that it is always shaken, not built. Many bartenders add egg white to give the drink more of froth at the finish. This makes it a Silver Fizz. Add egg yolk to make a Golden Fizz.

Pour the spirits and the lemon juice and gomme syrup into a shaker. Shake sharply. Strain into the glass and finish with soda water. Garnish with a slice of lemon and serve with a stirrer.

METHOD : shake
GLASS : highball

5cl/1 3/4oz gin
juice of half a lemon (if you like it sharper, use a whole lemon)
dash gomme syrup
soda water

Opposite
The Oasis Room at the Waldorf, 1934 – more refined than most watering-holes.

GODFATHER

METHOD : build
GLASS : old-fashioned

4cl/1 1/2oz Scotch whisky
2cl/2/3oz Amaretto

There's a family of these drinks – the Godmother is vodka based and the Godchild is brandy based (and it is also known as French Connection) – but they each contain Amaretto, an Italian almond/apricot-flavoured liqueur. This is an after-dinner drink.

Pour ingredients into the glass and stir. Serve with a stirrer.

GOLDEN CADILLAC

METHOD : shake
GLASS : cocktail

3cl/1oz Galliano
3cl/1oz white crême de cacao
3cl/1oz fresh cream

One of the best after-dinner cocktails. Made with Galliano, the drink has a gorgeous golden hue.

Pour ingredients into a shaker. Shake sharply and strain into the glass. ***Page 81.***

Golden Dawn

This pre-dinner cocktail won the International Cocktail Competition in London in 1930. Nine years later, Walter A. Madigan made a Golden Dawn without the Calvados and was runner-up at the International Cocktail Championship of the World in London in 1939.

Pour all of the ingredients except the grenadine into a shaker. Shake sharply. Strain into the glass and add a dash of grenadine. This gives the effect of a glorious sunrise, hence "Golden Dawn".

Method : shake
Glass : cocktail

The original recipe:
2cl/2/3oz gin
2cl/2/3oz apricot brandy
2cl/2/3oz Calvados
2cl/2/3oz fresh orange juice
dash of grenadine

Golden Dream

An after-dinner drink that was created in 1960 as a vehicle for the then "new" liqueur, Galliano.

Pour all ingredients into a shaker, shake sharply and strain into the glass.

Method : shake
Glass : cocktail

2cl/2/3oz Galliano
1.5cl/1/2oz Cointreau
1.5cl/1/2oz orange juice
1cl/1/3oz fresh cream

uinness

Grasshopper

This cocktail, with a creamy, mint flavour, is a good after-dinner drink. Hopefully, you will not leap after drinking this mixture.

Pour ingredients into the shaker and shake sharply. Strain into the glass.

Method : shake
Glass : cocktail

3cl/1oz green crême de menthe
3cl/1oz white crême de cacao
3cl/1oz fresh cream

Guinness Cooler

A delicious drink with an unusual mixture of sweetness and bitterness, with a hint of orange and coffee flavour.

Pour the Dubonnet, Kahlua and then Cointreau into the glass, finishing with the Guinness. Stir to create a head. Serve with a stirrer.

Method : build (no ice)
Glass : pilsener

2cl/2/3oz Dubonnet
1.5cl/1/2oz Kahlua
1.5cl/1/2oz Cointreau
15cl/5 1/2oz Guinness

Opposite
A 1958 Guinness poster by graphic designer Abram Games.

Harvey Wallbanger

Method : build
Glass : highball

5cl/1 3/4oz vodka
15cl/5 1/2oz fresh orange juice
2cl/2/3oz Galliano

An apocryphal tale surrounds the origins of the name of this well-known cocktail. Harvey was the name of a surfer who wiped out wildly in a surf championship and then soothed his wounded ego by drinking too much vodka and Galliano at Pancho's Bar, Manhattan Beach, California. At which point he banged his head against the wall and required friends to stop his self-destruction. This was in the 1960s when Smirnoff was in the midst of creating a young market for vodka in the USA, so whether it is a true tale or an urban myth – who knows?

Right
Harvey Wallbanger (left), Summer Scene (centre) and Raffles Singapore Sling (right).

Pour the vodka and the orange juice into the glass. Stir, then gently pour the Galliano over the back of a bar spoon. Garnish with a slice of orange. Add a stirrer and a straw.

THE HIGHBALL

Now as much a part of the American psyche as baseball, this popular 1920s cocktail was first created in 1895 by New York bartender Patrick Duffy. The name apparently originates from the railroad signalman's practise of raising a ball on a pole to urge a train driver to speed up – and speed is the essence in a highball. It usually consists of just two ingredients – one spirit and one mixer, originally soda. In the 1930s, a dash of bitters, Grenadine or Triple Sec and any of the sparkling mixers was an acceptable combination.

HORSE'S NECK

METHOD : build
GLASS : highball

5cl/1¾oz brandy
ginger ale
Angostura bitters (optional)

The original recipe for this highball was non-alcoholic and consisted of lemon peel, ice and ginger ale. But around 1910, bourbon was added. Other spirits were also used, of which brandy is now the most popular.

Pour the brandy into the glass. Top it up with ginger ale and add two dashes of Angostura bitters if required. Then cut the rind of a lemon in one spiral shape and place the end of the spiral over the edge of the glass and stretch the spiral down to the bottom of the glass.

HOT DRINKS

Hot drinks give one a sense of warmth and security. They are a late night drink, designed to calm the body down and prepare it for rest.

Some hot drinks, such as toddies, were originally medicinal, designed to cure colds and influenzas. They contain a slice of lemon or lemon juice, cinnamon, cloves and nutmeg, and can be made with any dark spirit although Scotch is the most popular.

HOT BUTTERED RUM

A true classic with a spicy finish.

Mix the butter, brown sugar, cinnamon, nutmeg and vanilla essence in the glass until it is creamy. Pour in the rum and the boiling water over a teaspoon and mix well. Some recipes recommend cloves but I prefer to use vanilla essence as it gives the drink a more pleasant nose. If you are on a diet, think of this as a special treat.

METHOD : build
GLASS : wine glass

5cl/1¾oz dark rum
1 small slice of butter
1 teaspoon brown sugar
cinnamon
nutmeg
vanilla essence
boiling water

Hot Scotch Toddy

Method : build
Glass : heat-resistant, with a handle

5cl/1¾oz Scotch whisky
7cl/2½oz boiling water
juice of half a lemon
3 dashes of Angostura bitters
1 teaspoon honey (or caster sugar)
2-3 cloves
twist of lemon

The origins of the name "toddy" are unclear. One suggestion is that it comes from "tarrie", a 17th-century word for a drink made in the East Indies from palm tree sap. The name reached England on the lips of returning sailors. In 1721, a Scottish poet, Allan Ramsey, made the rival claim that the name derived from Tod's Well, a source of Edinburgh water.

Pour the boiling water into the glass with the whisky, Angostura bitters and lemon juice. Spear the cloves into the twist of lemon and add. Stir to dissolve the honey (sugar) and serve.

Right
A 1941 advertisement for Johnny Walker, the world's best-selling Scotch whisky.

Good work—
Good whisky
Red Label
SPECIAL
Old Highland Whisky
JOHN WALKER & SONS, KILMARNOCK
ON HIS MAJESTY'S SERVICE
AUSTRALIA
WAR
CERTIFICATE
D 501369
ONE POUND
JW-105-15
JOHNNIE WALKER
Born 1820—still going strong
JOHN WALKER & SONS LTD., LONDON, KILMARNOCK, SYDNEY

IRISH COFFEE

METHOD : build
GLASS : wine goblet

2 teaspoons of brown sugar
5cl/1¾oz Irish whiskey
10cl/3½oz hot coffee
2cl/⅔oz whipped cream

The original recipe was created shortly after World War Two by Joe Sheridan, head bartender at Shannon Airport, near Ireland's Atlantic coast. The airport was a refuelling stop for aircraft and passengers alike. Joe took the traditional Irish drink, whiskey in tea, and made it more attractive to the American stop-over visitors by substituting coffee for tea, adding sugar, and topping it all off with a layer of lightly whipped Irish cream. This concoction was then served in a stemmed glass to take advantage of the contrast in colours.

The late Stanton Delaplane, a columnist for the San Francisco Chronicle, brought the recipe for Irish coffee to his favourite bar – the Buena Vista at Fisherman's Wharf, San Francisco. There is a bronze plaque on the wall outside the restaurant that records the fact that the first Irish coffee was served there in 1952. Now, more than 2000 Irish coffees are served there each day.

Pour the whisky into the goblet, add the sugar and stir. Add the hot coffee and stir with a silver spoon. Gently float the lightly whipped cream by pouring it the over the back of the spoon. Do not stir.

MORE LIQUEUR COFFEE DRINKS

There are many other different after-dinner coffee combinations, such as Royale Coffee – made with cognac; Italian coffee – made with Strega; Calypso Coffee – made with Tia Maria; Mexican Coffee – made with Kahlua; Caribbean Coffee – made with rum, and Royal Mint Coffee made with Royal Mint Chocolate Liqueur. These are each made the same way as an Irish Coffee.

Island Affair

Not only does this drink look fabulous, it also has an exotic tropical taste, with a hint of melon and coconut finish.

Pour the blue Curaçao, then the Midori, then the Cointreau into the glass. Gently add the mango and orange juice. Float the coconut cream on top. The drink will have layers of colour from the bottom to the top. Or you can stir the combination (before adding the coconut cream) to give it a green/blue tinge. Garnish with a slice of star fruit or a Cape gooseberry.

Method : build
Glass : highball

3cl/1oz Midori melon liqueur
1.5cl/1/2oz Cointreau
1.5cl/1/2oz blue Curaçao
5cl/1 3/4oz fresh orange juice
5cl/1 3/4oz mango juice
3cl/1oz coconut cream

Opposite
Island Affair with a Cape gooseberry garnish.

Jack Rose

A sharp and fruity drink that is reminiscent of Mr Jack Rose, the 1920s New York gangster, after whom it was allegedly named.

Pour ingredients into a shaker. Shake sharply and strain into the glass.

Method : shake
Glass : cocktail

5cl/1 3/4oz Applejack or Calvados
2cl/2/3oz fresh lime juice
1cl/1/3oz Grenadine

Kamikaze

Method : shake
Glass : old-fashioned/ cocktail

4cl/1 1/2oz vodka
2cl/2/3oz Cointreau
2cl/2/3oz fresh lime juice

A modern version of the Balalaika. The change of name, and the change of lemon to lime, has made it more popular than the original. Some recipes call for lime cordial, but I think the juice of a fresh lime is more refreshing.

Place all the ingredients into a shaker. Shake sharply and strain into the glass. Add a wedge of lime into the drink. Add a stirrer and serve.

Kir Royale

Method : build
Glass : flute

1cl/1/3oz crême de cassis
champagne

Cassis has a blackcurrant flavour and was added to Bourgogne Aligote wine by farm workers in Burgundy, France, to make it more drinkable. They named the drink after the war hero and Mayor of Dijon, Canon Felix Kir (1876-1968). When the wine was replaced by champagne the Kir was given a more fitting regal name.

Opposite
Black Velvet (left) and Kir Royale (right).

Pour the crême de cassis into the glass. Fill slowly with champagne.

LONG ISLAND ICED TEA

METHOD : build
GLASS : highball

1cl/1/3oz Bacardi
1cl/1/3oz gin
1cl/1/3oz vodka
1cl/1/3oz Cointreau
1cl/1/3oz tequila
juice of 1 lime
chilled cola

There are many versions of this drink. Even the early versions vary but basically it was made of five white spirits: white rum, vodka, gin, tequila and Cointreau. Some recipes do not include the vodka, others choose to omit the tequila.

Place all the ingredients into the glass. Stir. Finish by adding the chilled cola. Garnish with a wedge of lime on the edge of the glass. Add straw, stirrer and serve.

Opposite
A 1929 French poster uses the allure of three pairs of long legs to promote cocktails.

17
JEUX DE BAR
FANTASI
LE CHOIX D'UN COCKTAIL
EDOUARD BERNARD

MAI TAI

METHOD : shake
GLASS : highball/ goblet

2cl/2/3oz dark rum
2cl/2/3oz golden rum
1cl/1/3oz triple sec (or Cointreau)
1cl/1/3oz Orgeat (almond) syrup
juice of 1 lime
2-3 dashes Grenadine

Literally interpreted from Tahitian, the name means "the best". There are two rival claimants to its creation: Don Beach at Don the Beachcomber restaurant in Hollywood in the early 1930s; and "Trader" Vic in 1944. The Beach story is unauthenticated and until it is proven, Trader Vic must be given the credit.

He mixed a concoction of 17-year-old dark Jamaican rum, the juice of a fresh lime, a few dashes of Dutch orange Curaçao, French orgeat and rock candy syrup. After vigorously shaking it, he filled a glass with shaved ice and garnished it with a wedge of half a lime and a sprig of mint. Two friends from Tahiti were presented with the cocktail and, after a sip, one pronounced it to be: "Mai tai – roa ae" meaning "Out of this world – the best."

Pour ingredients into a shaker. Shake sharply and strain into the highball glass. Garnish with a nasturtium flower or a wedge of lime and a sprig of mint set on the rim of the glass. Add a straw, a stirrer and serve.

MAIDEN'S PRAYER

In *The Savoy Cocktail Book* a wry comment accompanies this pre-dinner drink: "If at first you don't succeed, cry, cry again"...which leads me to think that this is the cocktail for when a romance has gone awry! Perhaps Harry had a tearful young lady at the bar and made her this mixture to cheer her up. I don't know if it worked – but the name of the drink remains one of the classics.

Place ingredients in a shaker. Shake sharply. Strain into the cocktail glass. Garnish with a twist of orange.

METHOD : shake
GLASS : cocktail

3cl/1oz gin
3cl/1oz Cointreau
1.5cl/½oz fresh orange juice
1.5cl/½oz fresh lemon juice

MANHATTAN

METHOD : mixing glass
GLASS : cocktail

5cl/1 3/4oz Canadian Club whisky
2cl/2/3oz sweet vermouth
1 dash Angostura bitters

A recipe for a Manhattan was published in some of the early 1880s bartenders' guides. Basically, it requires the addition of vermouth to a whisky cocktail.

The origins of the name are unclear – some say it was it created in 1874 at the Manhattan Club, New York, for Lady Randolph Churchill, who held a banquet there to honour the politican Samuel J. Tilden.

Today, the accepted recipe for this pre-dinner drink needs a sweet vermouth but there is another version, called a Dry Manhattan, which was more popular in the 1920s and 1930s, and also the Perfect Manhattan – a mixture of dry and sweet vermouth.

Place ingredients into the mixing glass and stir. Strain into the cocktail glass. Garnish with a Maraschino cherry. For a Dry Manhattan, a twist of lemon and for the Perfect Manhattan, a twist of orange and a Maraschino cherry. ***Page 113.***

Opposite
A cinematic cocktail of intrigue.

MANHATTAN
COCKTAIL
WITH
NANCY CARROLL
RICHARD ARLEN
and PAUL LUKAS
Directed by
DOROTHY ARZNER
Story by
ERNEST VAJDA
Screen play by
ETHEL DOHERTY
Morgan
a Paramount Picture
Paramount
Pictures

A TOAST TO MARGARITA ...

Stirring tribute, indeed! But then a Tequila Margarita with *Cuervo* invites uncommon praise . . . a cocktail for those unhurried moments when one can pause to relish properly each special rite of preparation, to anticipate each measured taste. Consider first the salting of the glass: Crystals thinly spread on a dry napkin, then the moistened champagne glass twirled lightly until just the rim is edged with salt. Next the Margarita—jigger of Jose Cuervo Tequila, juice of one lime, half jigger of Triple Sec—well-shaken with shaved ice and quickly poured. The moment at hand, you taste . . . slowly, consciously . . . *Muy simpático!* Surprised? You shouldn't be, for Cuervo Tequila is equally delightful in most cocktails. Pardon a suggestion, but we highly recommend a tequila martini, sour or the exotic tequila sunrise. With Cuervo, please . . . supreme quality for 150 years.

JOSE CUERVO TEQUILA

SOLE U.S. IMPORTERS YOUNG'S MARKET COMPANY, LOS ANGELES, CALIFORNIA

MARGARITA

METHOD : shake
GLASS : cocktail

3cl/1oz tequila
3cl/1oz fresh lime juice
2cl/2/3oz triple sec (or Cointreau)

One of the most well-known tequila-based pre-dinner cocktails and still one of the most requested. The name has intrigue, a hint of romance and femininity. American actress Marjorie King was the guest at Rancha La Gloria in Tijuana, Mexico, owned by Danny Herrera. When he discovered the actress was allergic to every spirit but tequila, he mixed this and named it Margarita – the Mexican equivalent of Marjorie.

A frozen margarita is served with crushed ice; the frozen fruit margarita is made in a blender with fresh fruit, a liqueur the flavour of the fruit and crushed ice.

Rub the rim of the glass with a wedge of lime and dip the rim into a saucer of fine salt. Place all ingredients into a shaker. Shake sharply and strain into the glass. Garnish with a wedge of lime on the rim of the glass.

Some recipes use a larger measure of tequila but I prefer this balance of tequila and lime because it gives the drink a more lip-smacking finish. ***Page 99.***

Opposite
A toast to the spirit from south of the border.

Mimosa

Method : build
Glass : flute

fresh orange juice
2 dashes Grand Marnier
champagne

A classic cocktail from 1925, created at the Ritz Hotel, Paris, it is named after the tropical flowering shrub. The combination of champagne and orange juice and Grand Marnier produces a similar colour to the Mimosa's sensitive yellow blooms.

Squeeze enough fresh orange juice to fill a quarter of the frosted flute. Add the Grand Marnier and finish with the champagne. Stir.

Daisy rose, smiling faintly, and went to the table.

"Open the whiskey, Tom," she ordered, "and I'll make you a mint julep. Then you won't seem so stupid to yourself..."

The Great Gatsby, F. Scott Fitzgerald, 1925

MINT JULEP

METHOD : build
GLASS : highball

4-5 fresh mint leaves
1 teaspoon caster sugar
5cl/1 3/4oz bourbon
1 tablespoon cold water

Now considered a refreshing summer drink, the mint julep originated from Virginia in the American South. The earliest record of the drink was in 1803, written by one John Davis, a British tutor working in the grand houses of Southern plantations. He defined a julep as "a dram of spirituous liquor that has mint in it, taken by Virginians of a morning". The Webster's American Dictionary refers to it as a "kind of liquid medicine".

The julep was introduced to England by sea captain and novelist Frederick Marryatt, who was as enamoured with it as he was with American ladies.

Place the mint in the highball glass. Add the sugar and water. Crush the mint with the back of a bar spoon until the sugar is dissolved and the fragrance of the mint is released. Add the bourbon. Fill the glass with crushed ice and stir. Place a sprig of mint on the rim of the glass. Add straw, stirrer and serve.

Moscow Mule

Method : build
Glass : highball

5cl/1¾oz Smirnoff vodka
2cl/⅔oz fresh lime juice
ginger beer

The idea for the Moscow Mule was generated in 1941 when Heublein & Co., USA, acquired the US rights to Smirnoff vodka on the West Coast. The company was looking for a way to compete with gin. An employee, John Martin, was at the Cock 'n' Bull Saloon in Los Angeles and the owner was complaining about being stuck with too much ginger beer. The two enterprising men mixed the new spirit with ginger beer, added a dash of lime juice – and created the Moscow Mule. As a gimmick it was originally served in a distinctive copper mug.

During the Second World War, Heublein suspended the campaign. In 1947, the cocktail was re-launched with a clever advertising slogan: "It leaves you breathless." that caught people's imagination. Some bartenders add just a small drop of Angostura bitters.

Opposite
Woody Allen came out of his shell to advertise Smirnoff vodka in the 60s.

Pour the vodka and lime juice into the glass. Finish with ginger beer. Garnish with a wedge of lime in the glass. Add a stirrer and serve. ***Page 87.***

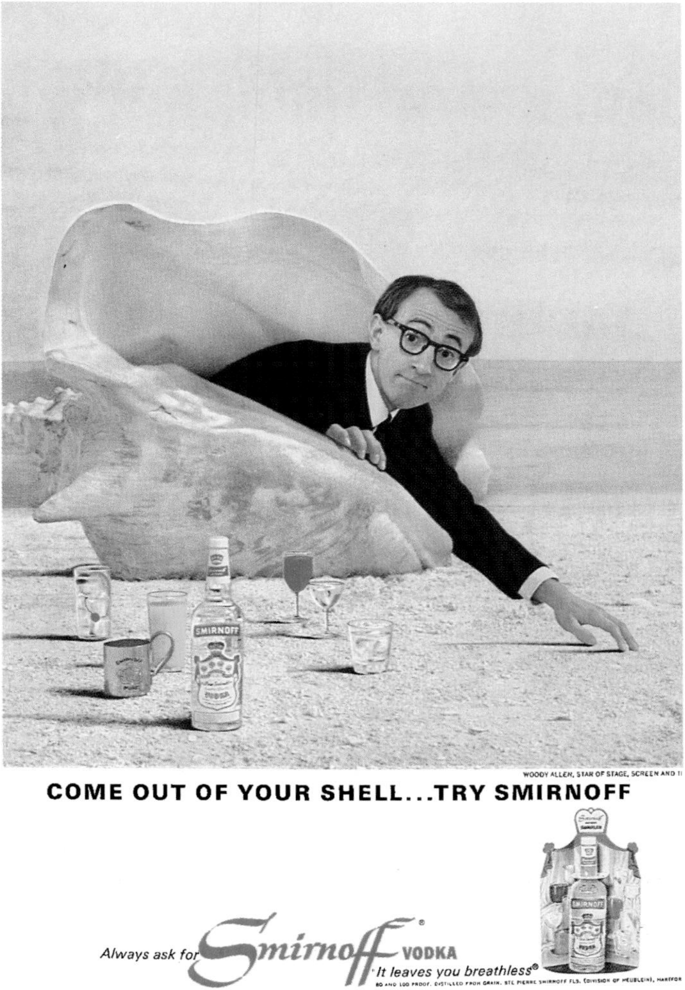

WOODY ALLEN, STAR OF STAGE, SCREEN AND T

COME OUT OF YOUR SHELL...TRY SMIRNOFF

CAMPARI ·

ITTER
CAMPARI
I più diffuso ed apprezzato degli aperitivi

DAVIDE CAMPARI & C.
MILANO
Stabilimento
SESTO S. GIOVANNI
(Milano

CORDIAL
CAMPARI

NEGRONI

This has the right balance of sweetness and bitterness to stimulate the appetite. To make it a long drink, add soda water. The name originates from a Florentine, Count Camillo Negroni, who regularly visited the Casoni Bar in Florence. The story goes that he ordered his usual Americano with a little gin and the resulting drink soon became known as the Negroni.

Pour ingredients into the glass. Stir, add soda if required. Garnish with a slice of orange in the drink. Add a stirrer and serve immediately.

METHOD : build
GLASS : old-fashioned

3cl/1oz Campari
3cl/1oz gin
3cl/1oz sweet vermouth
soda water (optional)

Opposite
A turn-of-the century Italian Campari advertisement.

OLD-FASHIONED

METHOD : build
GLASS : old-fashioned

5cl/1 3/4oz bourbon whiskey
1 dash Angostura bitters
1 white sugar cube
soda water

Colonel James E. Pepper, a Kentucky-based distiller of bourbon, and the bartender of the Pendennis Club, Louisville, were jointly responsible for the creation of this cocktail around 1900. Once referred to as a "palate-paralyser" by bartender David Embury, the old-fashioned is a cocktail with a song in its honour, *Make It Another Old-Fashioned, Please* by Cole Porter. The name is also associated with a glass and hence is always on someone's lips.

Place the sugar cube in the glass and soak the sugar with the Angostura bitters. Add a splash of soda (to cover the sugar cube) and crush the cube with the back of the bar spoon. Add the whiskey, then fill the glass. Stir and garnish with a slice of orange and a Maraschino cherry, and add a twist of lemon. ***Page 78.***

PIMM'S NO 1.

This is a bitter, fruit drink with a dry-gin base. Served as a cup, Pimm's No. 1 is the original and most popular gin-sling. Pimm's became the ladies' drink of the 1950s and 60s, no doubt helped along by its marketing as an elegant society drink.

This is the only pre-mixed cocktail that is used by a professional bartender.

Prepare by pouring the Pimm's into a highball glass with ice cubes. Add lemonade or ginger ale. Garnish with a slice of lemon and orange, the rind of a cucumber and a sprig of fresh mint in the drink. Some bartenders use a lot more fruit, which can detract from the taste of the Pimm's mixture.

For the adventurous in spirit, replace the lemonade with champagne – this makes a Pimm's Royale.

METHOD : build
GLASS : highball

5cl/1 3/4oz Pimm's No. 1 cup
lemonade or ginger ale
lemon and orange slices
cucumber rind
sprig of fresh mint

PIÑA COLADA

METHOD : blender
GLASS : colada/goblet

5cl/1 3/4oz Bacardi (or white rum)
10cl/3 1/2oz pineapple juice (or three slices of canned pineapple)
5cl/1 3/4oz coconut cream
crushed ice

The most famous of the coladas is the Piña Colada – meaning "strained pineapple". There is no doubt that this glamorous drink originated in Puerto Rico but two bartenders claim to have invented the recipe. One is Ramon Marrero Perez of the Caribe Hilton, who claims he mixed the first Piña Colada in 1954; the other is Don Ramon Portas Mingot of La Barrachina Restaurant Bar in 1963. As with many of these cocktails, it is an matter of on-going contention, as rarely is a recipe written down at the time.

There are many different ways to create a Piña Colada. Some bartenders use pineapple juice from a can; others use the juice and fibre from pineapple that has been crushed in a blender.

A Piña Colada should be smooth and easy to drink. It is important to use the highest quality and freshest pineapple juice you can find. When made, the whole drink should be snow-white in colour, not separated into clear liquid and froth. Some bartenders like to use two rums – light and dark.

Pour the pineapple juice (or three slices of canned pineapple) into the blender, add the coconut cream and the white rum. Blend for a few seconds. Add the crushed ice and blend for 5 seconds. Pour into a large goblet or colada glass. The most common garnish is a quarter slice of fresh pineapple (try not to cut it too thick) skewered with a red Maraschino cherry. I prefer to use a more simple garnish such as a slice of star fruit on the rim of the glass. Serve with a straw. ***Page 105.***

TIP: *If you want more texture in the drink – without it being too grainy – you can use a good quality can of sliced pineapple. They are softer, blend more easily and are sweeter. I learnt this from two superb bartenders, Charlie and Daniel, at Little Dix Bay in the British Virgin Islands. Thanks, guys.*

PINK GIN

Angostura bitters was perfected as a remedy for stomach complaints by Dr Johann G. B. Siegert, who used plant extracts and named it after the Venezuelan town of Angostura on the Orinoco River. Word of this medicine reached the British Navy, who added it not only to their medicine kit, but also to their Plymouth gin rations. Hence "Pink" gin. Some prefer it with a splash of iced water; others like it straight.

Pour gin and bitters into mixing glass and stir. Strain into the cocktail glass.

METHOD : mixing glass
GLASS : cocktail/ old-fashioned

5cl/1¾oz gin
1–2 dashes Angostura Bitters

Pink Lady

Method : shake
Glass : cocktail

5cl/1 3/4oz gin
1-2 dashes Grenadine
1 egg white
2cl/2/3oz lemon juice

A good Plymouth gin-based pre-dinner cocktail named after a successful 1912 stage play, it has a pomegranate flavour.

Pour all ingredients into a shaker. Shake sharply. Strain into the glass and garnish with a red Maraschino cherry.

Planter's Punch

Method : shake
Glass : highball

5cl/1 3/4oz Myers's dark rum
15cl/5 1/2oz orange juice
juice of 1 lime
2 dashes Grenadine
1 dash gomme syrup (or caster sugar)

A drink created in Jamaica to celebrate the opening of Myers's Rum distillery in 1879. The fame of Fred L. Myers's cocktail mixture spread quickly through the island (particularly at Kelly's Bar on Sugar Wharf), and on to the rest of the world. The original recipe, and a modern version, follow.

Planter's Punch No 1 (The Original)

Pour all ingredients into a shaker, shake sharply and strain into the glass. Garnish with a slice of orange, a red Maraschino cherry and a sprig of mint.

PLANTER'S PUNCH No.2

Pour all ingredients except the dark rum into a shaker. Shake sharply and strain into the glass. Carefully float the dark rum on top of the drink. Garnish with a slice of orange, a red Maraschino cherry and a sprig of mint sitting on the rim of the glass.

Some Planter's Punch recipes contain dark or mixed rum, lemon juice, Grenadine and soda water.

METHOD : shake
GLASS : colada/goblet

2cl/2/3oz white rum
2cl/2/3oz dark rum
1cl/1/3oz Cointreau or triple sec
5cl/1 3/4oz pineapple juice
5cl/1 3/4oz orange juice
juice of a lime
1-2 dashes Grenadine

PRAIRIE OYSTER

An ancient hangover cure guaranteed to settle the worst headache and an awful, upset stomach.

Rinse the glass with olive oil and throw away the oil. Add the tomato ketchup, and the egg yolk (do not break the egg yolk) and season with the Worcestershire sauce, vinegar and salt and pepper to taste. Close your eyes and drink in one gulp. Think about the pleasure you had the night before. Serve a small glass of ice water on the side.

METHOD : build (no ice)
GLASS : small wine glass

virgin olive oil
1 egg yolk
1-2 tablespoons of tomato ketchup
salt and ground black pepper
dash Worcestershire sauce
dash white wine vinegar

Pussyfoot

Method : shake
Glass : highball

juice of 1 lemon
juice of 1 lime
15cl/5 1/2oz orange juice
1–2 dashes Grenadine
1 egg yolk

A non-alcoholic cocktail for guests who want to drive home afterwards.

Pour all ingredients into a shaker, shake sharply, and strain into the highball glass. Garnish with a slice of orange and a Maraschino cherry.

Pousse Café

Method : build (no ice)
Glass : shot

1cl/1/3oz Grenadine
1cl/1/3oz green crême de menthe
1cl/1/3oz Galliano
1cl/1/3oz Kummel
1cl/1/3oz brandy

Served after dinner, this cocktail consists of several liqueurs or spirits of specific gravities that sit in layers in the glass. The liqueurs must remain strictly separated, one above the other. Each liquor has a different density: basically syrups are heavier than liquors, spirits are lighter. Pour the heaviest liquid first. Formulas differ between manufacturers and consequently densities vary slightly.

You can use any colour combination you wish. If you want to celebrate a red, white and blue Fourth of July, use the Grenadine as a base, the Cointreau and then the blue Curaçao in equal parts. You can make it in advance and chill in the refrigerator.

POUSSE CAFÉ 81

Pour the Grenadine in as the base, then over the back of a bar spoon, slowly add crême de menthe, Galliano, Kummel and lastly, the brandy.

RAMOS FIZZ

In 1888 Henrico C. Ramos arrived in New Orleans, bought the Imperial Cabinet Saloon, and created a drink by mixing gin, caster sugar (superfine), orange-flower water, lemon and lime juices, egg white, cream, and seltzer water. In the shaker, the ingredients combined to create a light, mouth-watering, heavenly cocktail. The formula was a secret until the saloon was closed in 1920 at the beginning of Prohibition, and Henrico's brother, Charles Henry Ramos, let the world know the recipe.

METHOD : shake
GLASS : old-fashioned

5cl/1¾oz gin
juice of half a lime
juice of half a lemon
3 dashes orange-flower water
1 egg white
5cl/1¾oz single (light) cream
1 teaspoon caster sugar
soda water (optional)

Pour all of the ingredients except the soda into a shaker. Shake sharply. Strain into the glass with ice. Finish with soda water if required. Serve with a straw and a stirrer. Garnish with a wedge of lime sitting on the edge of the glass, and a sprig of mint.

Rickey

Method : build
Glass : highball

5cl/1 3/4oz gin
juice of 1 lime
soda water

The original gin rickey was allegedly created for an American lobbyist, Joe Rickey, at Shoemaker's Restaurant in Washington DC, 1893. The bartender at Shoemaker's squeezed limes into gin and squirted a soda syphon over the concoction. You can make a Rickey using any spirit as a base; vodka is becoming more popular for this drink. A Rickey is a close cousin of the Collins and the Fizz – the difference being it contains no sugar.

Pour the gin and lime into a glass. Finish with soda water and stir. Garnish with a wedge of lime.

Road Runner

Method : shake
Glass : cocktail

4cl/1 1/2oz vodka
2cl/2/3oz Amaretto
2cl/2/3oz coconut cream

An after-dinner digestif with an almond and coconut finish.

Pour all ingredients into a shaker and shake sharply. Strain into the glass and garnish with a Cape gooseberry and a dusting of nutmeg. ***Page 171.***

Rob Roy

The only cocktail to imbibe on Saint Andrew's Day, it takes its name from the Scottish rebel hero, Rob Roy.

Pour the ingredients into the mixing glass and stir. Strain into the glass and garnish with a Maraschino cherry. I prefer a twist of orange – it gives the drink extra zest.

Method : mixing glass
Glass : cocktail

4cl/1 1/2oz Scotch whisky
4cl/1 1/2oz sweet vermouth
1-2 dashes Angostura bitters

Rusty Nail

Pour the whisky into the glass, add the Drambuie and stir it well. Garnish with a twist of lemon.

Method : build
Glass : old-fashioned

5cl/1 3/4oz Scotch whisky
3cl/1oz Drambuie

Salty Dog

A close relation to the Greyhound, this is a pre-dinner drink.

Pour the ingredients into a shaker. Shake sharply. Rub a wedge of lemon around the rim of the glass and dip it into a saucer of salt. Strain the mixture into the glass.

Method : shake
Glass : cocktail

4cl/1 1/2oz vodka
4cl/1 1/2oz fresh grapefruit juice

Sazerac

Method : build
Glass : old-fashioned

5cl/1 3/4oz bourbon whiskey
dash Angostura bitters or Peychaud bitters
1 cube white sugar
1cl/1/3oz absinthe (Pernod)
soda water

A cocktail that made its film debut with the suave hero James Bond in *Live and Let Die*. Some recommend this short drink as an aphrodisiac.

Place the sugar cube in the glass and soak with bitters. Add a splash of soda to cover the sugar and crush with the back of the bar spoon. Add the bourbon whiskey, stir and float the Pernod over the top. Garnish with a twist of lemon.

Screwdriver

Method : build
Glass : highball

5cl/1 3/4oz vodka
15cl/5 1/2oz fresh orange juice

A relatively new long drink created in the 1950s, the legend evolved when an American oilman in Iran allegedly stirred this combination with a screwdriver. Make it quickly and always use fresh orange juice to bring out the full flavour.

Pour the vodka into the glass. Add the orange juice and stir. Serve with a stirrer and garnish with a slice of orange.

Right
The last person in need of an aphrodisiac.

HARRY SALTZMAN and ALBERT R BROCCOLI present
ROGER MOORE as JAMES BOND
007
in IAN FLEMING'S
"LIVE AND LET DIE"
DEVIL
DEATH
LOVERS
FORTUNE
with
YAPHET KOTTO · JANE SEYMOUR · Produced by HARRY SALTZMAN and ALBERT R BROCCOLI · Directed by GUY HAMILTON
Screenplay by TOM MANKIEWICZ · Title Song Composed by PAUL and LINDA McCARTNEY and Sung by PAUL McCARTNEY and WINGS
Music Score by GEORGE MARTIN · COLOR
MGM/UA

SEA BREEZE

METHOD : build
GLASS : highball

5cl/1¾oz vodka
10cl/3½oz cranberry juice
5cl/1¾oz fresh grapefruit juice

This long drink makes the top 10 list of vodka-based drinks. In the 1930s, a Sea Breeze contained gin, apricot brandy, Grenadine and lemon juice; a later recipe contained vodka, dry vermouth, Galliano and blue Curaçao. But it's this combination of vodka, cranberry and grapefruit juice that is considered to be the classic Sea Breeze today.

Pour the ingredients into the glass. Stir. Garnish with a wedge of lime and serve with a stirrer. ***Page 81.***

SHIRLEY TEMPLE

METHOD : build
GLASS : highball

ginger ale (or Seven-Up)
2-3 dashes Grenadine

This "mocktail" – named after the child actress – is a sweet-tasting, long drink that became the clichéd non-alcholic cocktail of the 1960s and 70s.

Pour the ginger ale into a glass, add the Grenadine and stir. Serve with a stirrer and a straw. Garnish with 2–3 red Maraschino cherries.

Left

Liquori Galliano, named after a courageous Italian major, was once a key element of the Sea Breeze. It is now more famous for its walk-on part in the Harvey Wallbanger.

Sidecar

Created by Harry at Harry's New York Bar, Paris, after the First World War for an eccentric Captain who turned up in a chauffeur-driven motorbike sidecar.

Pour ingredients into a shaker. Shake sharply. Strain into the glass.

Method : shake
Glass : cocktail

3cl/1oz brandy
2cl/2/3oz Cointreau
2cl/2/3oz fresh lemon juice

Opposite
Sidecar (left) and Cosmopolitan (right).

Silver Bullet

A pre-1930s short drink with a fennel and juniper flavour. Originally it was made with gin but it is more common now to use vodka as a base. The original recipe is first.

Pour the ingredients into the shaker. Shake sharply. Strain into glass and serve.

Method : shake
Glass : cocktail

4cl/1 1/2oz gin
2cl/2/3oz Kummel
1cl/1/3oz fresh lemon juice

Vodka Silver Bullet

Pour ingredients into the mixing glass. Stir, strain into the glass and serve.

Method : mixing glass
Glass : cocktail

4cl/1 1/2oz vodka
3cl/1oz Kummel

Singapore Sling

Method : shake
Glass : highball

The most commonly used recipe for a Singapore Sling bears little resemblance to the original Singapore Sling created by Ngiam Tong Boon, a bartender at Raffles Hotel, Singapore, in 1915.

Originally intended as a woman's drink, this long, exotic drink is now enjoyed by both sexes.

The original legendary cocktail was a favourite of, among others, the famous writers Somerset Maugham and Joseph Conrad, and actor Douglas Fairbanks.

Raffles Singapore Sling

2cl/⅔oz gin
2cl/⅔oz cherry brandy
1cl/⅓oz Cointreau
1cl/⅓oz Benedictine
1cl/⅓oz fresh lime juice
7cl/2½oz fresh orange juice
7cl/2½oz pineapple juice

Pour ingredients into a shaker. Shake sharply. Strain into the glass. Garnish with a slice of pineapple and a Maraschino cherry. Add a straw and a stirrer. Use a bright cherry brandy to ensure a pinker finish. ***Page 121.***

Singapore Sling

4cl/1½oz gin
2cl/⅔oz cherry brandy
2cl/⅔oz fresh lemon juice
soda water

Place all ingredients but the soda into a shaker. Shake sharply. Strain into the glass. Finish with soda water. Garnish with a slice of lemon and a red Maraschino cherry.

SNOWBALL

METHOD : build
GLASS : highball

5cl/1¾oz Advocaat
2cl/⅔oz Rose's Lime cordial
lemonade

In *The Savoy Cocktail Book* Harry Craddock refers to this drink in a rather scathing manner: "This is woman's work." What he means is that no self-respecting macho man would request this delicious but rather feminine low-alcohol drink. Harry's recipe was entirely different from what we now know as the Snowball today. This is the Snowball that was at the height of its popularity in Europe in the late 1960s – so popular, in fact, that a battery-powered swizzle stick was manufactured especially for this drink.

Another version of the Snowball was created for the Earl of Northesk, the famous English bobsleigh champion. It contained gin, crême de violette, white crême de menthe, anisette and sweet cream – not the same cocktail at all.

Pour ingredients into the glass. Stir vigorously, making sure the Advocaat is mixed in well.

Stinger

Method : build
Glass : old-fashioned

4cl/1 1/2oz brandy
2cl/3/4oz white crême de menthe

Originally served straight-up in pre-Prohibition days, most people request it on the rocks in an old-fashioned glass. It is a pleasant after-dinner drink – the brandy and the crême de menthe acting together as a soothing digestive.

Pour the brandy, then the crême de menthe over the ice in the glass. Stir and serve with a stirrer.

Tequila Sunrise

Method : build
Glass : highball

5cl/1 3/4oz tequila
1-2 dashes Grenadine
15cl/5 1/2oz fresh orange juice

A Mexican concoction created in the 1930s, this colourful long drink has maintained a certain *je ne sais quoi.*

Pour the orange and tequila into the glass and stir. Splash in the Grenadine so that it sinks slowly through the mixture, like the sun's rays. Garnish with a slice of orange and a Maraschino cherry. Serve with straw and a stirrer.

Tom and Jerry

A hot drink invented by "Professor" Jerry Thomas in 1852 at the Planter's House Bar, St Louis, Missouri. When he moved to New York, Manhattanites found the cocktail to their liking. The Professor refused to serve the drink before the first snowfall – making this, and the Blue Blazer, the classic cold weather drinks of that era.

Beat the egg yolk and the white separately, then mix them together in the glass. Add the spirits and sugar and fill with boiling water (or hot milk if you prefer). Grate fresh nutmeg over the top and serve.

Method : build
Glass : heat-resistant toddy

1 egg
3.5cl/1 1/4oz dark rum
1.5cl/1/2oz brandy
1 teaspoon caster sugar

Tom Collins

Method : build
Glass : highball

juice of 1 lemon
5cl/1 3/4oz gin
1–2 dashes gomme syrup
soda water

The original Collins was a John Collins and can be traced back to the head waiter at Limmer's, a popular hotel and coffee house in Conduit Street, London around 1790–1817. His original recipe uses genever, a Dutch-style gin. The drink was not that popular in America in the 1880s, where it was regarded as an upmarket type of gin sling. When one bartender used Old Tom Gin (a London gin with a sweet flavour), the Collins became much more popular and henceforth it was known as a Tom Collins.

It is now accepted that the Collins is made with London gin, although you can use any other spirit (brandy, rum, whisky). In America, a John Collins is made with bourbon or whisky.

Right
Sisterly advice to head for the gin cupboard – purely for medicinal reasons, of course.

Add lemon juice, gomme syrup and gin to the glass. Finish with soda water. Stir. Garnish with a slice of lemon in the drink and serve with stirrer.

"My dear –
Why don't you do as I tell you? Go and get a drop of **Gordon's** out of the bottle in the sideboard. You will find it will put you right at once, and is far more pleasant to take"
Gordon's
THE GIN THAT HAS MEDICINAL PROPERTIES
TANQUERAY, GORDON & CO. LTD., GIN DISTILLERS, LONDON

Velvet Hammer

Method : shake
Glass : cocktail

3cl/1oz Tia Maria
3cl/1oz Cointreau
3cl/1oz fresh cream

Softly, softly into the night with this after-dinner drink – to sip it is to caress the palate with velvet.

Pour all ingredients into the shaker and shake sharply. Strain into the glass and serve immediately.

Whiskey Sour

Method : shake
Glass : cocktail

5cl/1 3/4oz bourbon whiskey
2cl/2/3oz fresh lemon juice
1 egg white
dash gomme syrup

The original sour – a brandy sour – was a favourite drink in the 1850s and it remains popular today. You can make sours with any spirit but the most requested is a whiskey sour. Fresh juices are essential to provide the sour flavour of the drink.

Pour all ingredients into a shaker. Shake sharply. Strain into the glass. Garnish with a red Maraschino cherry and a slice of orange.

Right
"Canadian Club" – the same in any langauge.

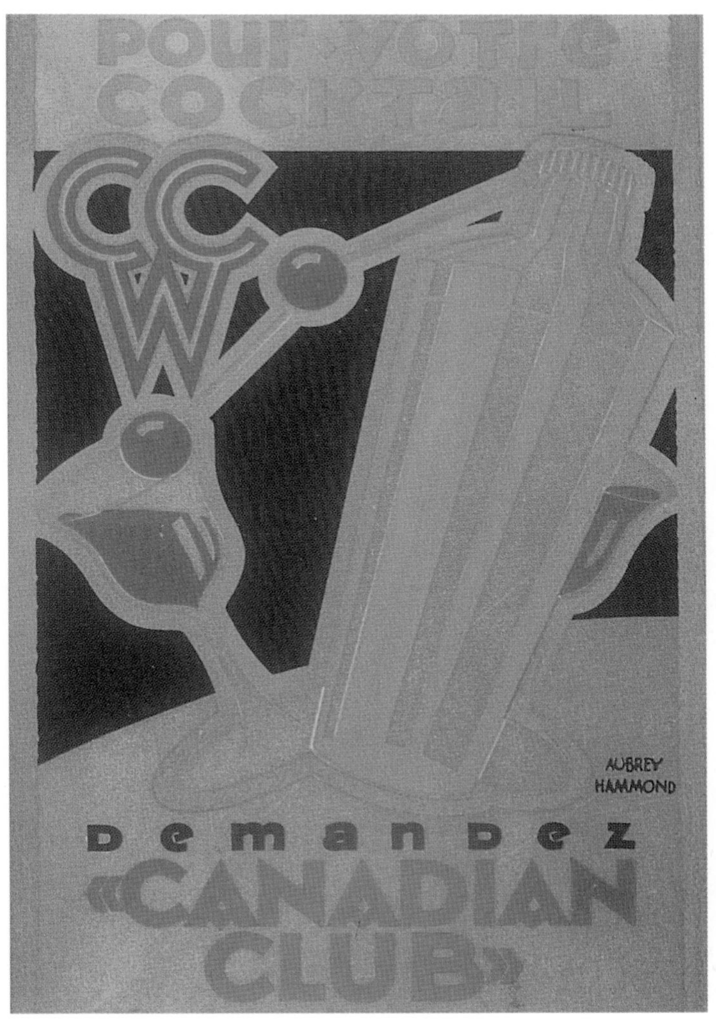
AUBREY
HAMMOND
demandez
«CANADIAN
CLUB»

White Lady

Method : shake
Glass : cocktail

3cl/1oz gin
3cl/1oz Cointreau
3cl/1oz fresh lemon juice

Created by legendary bartender Harry MacElhone while at Ciro's Club, London in 1919. The perfect balance of sweetness and sharpness makes this an ideal pre-dinner drink.

Pour ingredients into the shaker. Shake sharply and strain into the glass.

White Russian

Method : build
Glass : old-fashioned

4cl/1 1/2oz vodka
2cl/2/3oz Kahlua
2cl/2/3oz lightly whipped cream

The only difference between this and a Black Russian is that this contains cream, hence the whiteness. An excellent after-dinner drink.

Pour the vodka, then the Kahlua, into the glass, stir, then gently float the cream on top. Serve with a stirrer.

Opposite
White Russian (left), Road Runner (centre) and B-52 (right).

Right
Fly to the Caribbean on a Yellow Bird.

YELLOW BIRD

A short, vibrant, exotic drink that is popular in the Caribbean.

Pour all ingredients into a shaker, shake sharply, and strain into the glass. Garnish with a thin slice of orange and a spiral of lime on the rim of the glass.

METHOD : shake
GLASS : cocktail

3cl/1oz white rum
1.5cl/1/2oz Cointreau
1.5cl/1/2oz Galliano
1.5cl/1/2oz lime juice

ZOMBIE

An exotic cocktail dating from 1934, when it was created by Don Beach at Don the Beachcomber restaurant in Hollywood. Made for a guest suffering from a hangover who reportedly used the words "like a zombie" when asked what he felt like. This is the original recipe...but it has since undergone many transformations as it has travelled from bar to bar.

Pour all ingredients except the 151 proof rum into the shaker. Shake sharply. Strain into the glass filled with dry crushed ice. Float the 151 proof rum on top. Garnish with a slice of orange and lime and a sprig of mint. Add a straw and a stirrer.

METHOD : shake
GLASS : highball

1.5cl/1/2oz white rum
1.5cl/1/2oz golden rum
1.5cl/1/2oz dark rum
1cl/1/3oz cherry brandy
1cl/1/3oz apricot brandy
5cl/1 3/4oz pineapple juice
3cl/1oz orange juice
1cl/1/3oz lime juice
2cl/2/3oz papaya juice
dash almond syrup
dash 151 proof Demerara rum (high proof rum)

Calabrese Classics

Opposite
Lady Hunt (left) and Anouchka (right).

Here are just a few of the cocktails that I have created for special occasions. Some use unexpected ingredients – such as a yellow pepper – others use common ingredients in an unexpected way. Each of these recipes is a combination of eye-catching colours and a lip-smacking blend of sweetness and sharpness.

Anouchka

Method : mixing glass
Glass : cocktail

7cl/2½oz vodka
1cl/⅓oz crême de mure (blackberry liqueur)

Named after a beautiful Russian guest who requested something strong and sweet. As I was busy at the time, I made her this drink instead...

Pour the vodka into mixing glass and add the crême de mure. Stir and strain into the glass. The drink will be lilac in colour.

Blood Transfusion

Method : build
Glass : highball

3cl/1oz vodka
3cl/1oz dry sherry
3cl/1oz Fernet-Branca
15cl/5½oz tomato juice
1–2 dashes of Worcestershire sauce
pinch of celery salt
juice of 1 lime

A drink to clear the head if you are suffering from a hangover. People react to alcohol in different ways. With some people, it is the stomach, and to settle that you need something strong like Fernet-Branca (a bitter spirit). With others, it is the head and to cure that, you need plenty of juices and plenty of water to combat the dehydration from the alcohol.

Three-quarters fill the glass with ice cubes and pour the vodka and the sherry in first. Add the tomato and lime juice, then add the celery salt and Worcestershire sauce. Stir. Float a layer of the Fernet-Branca on top. It'll either cure you or kill you! The rest of the drink will sort out your head and make you forget the night before. Good luck.

CAMPARI NOBILE

A drink I created for the 1993 Campari Barman of the Year competition. As its name suggests, it is a noble drink, with the vodka balancing the bitter and sweet. Lemoncello is a traditional drink from Italy's Amalfi coast and brings the sunshine into the drink and your heart.

METHOD : shake
GLASS : highball

2cl/2/3oz vodka
2cl/2/3oz Campari
1cl/1/3oz lemon liqueur (Lemoncello)
10cl/3 1/2oz combination of fresh orange and raspberry juice
bitter lemon

Pour the juices into a shaker. Add the vodka, campari and the Lemoncello. Shake sharply. Strain into a highball glass. Finish the drink by adding bitter lemon and stir. To garnish: float four or five fresh raspberries on top of the drink, sit a twist of orange on the rim of the glass and add a fresh mint leaf in the middle of the raspberries. Add a straw and a stirrer. Now dream you are on the Amalfi Coast, one of the most beautiful coastlines in the world and my hometown. I am there already. ***Page 185.***

BITTER
CAMPARI
l'aperitivo

Cinnamon Warmer

This is smooth and easy to make. You can take this drink on a cold, misty morning before you face the world outside – its vitamins will invigorate your bloodstream. Or before you go out for a night on the town – it will fortify you against the elements. You know the saying: "An apple a day keeps the Doctor away." Well, here you have liquid apple.

Pour all of the liquid, including the honey, into a saucepan and heat slowly. Do not boil. Place the spices in a muslin cloth, tie the top in a knot and place in the saucepan. (This provides the flavour and avoids having to scoop the bits out when the drink is ready.) Float a few twists of lemon and orange peel in the mixture. This will give a slight citrus taste. Strain into the glass and enjoy.

Method : build
Glass : heat-resistant toddy

3.5cl/1 1/4oz Calvados (apple brandy)
1.5cl/1/2oz dark rum
10cl/3 1/2oz clear apple juice
juice of half a lemon
3 thin slices of fresh ginger
1 teaspoon clear honey
3 cloves
1 small cinnamon stick

Left
An early advertisement for Campari.

GG

Method : shake
Glass : highball

3cl/1oz Bombay Sapphire gin
2cl/2/3oz Midori
1cl/1/3oz blue Curaçao
juice of half a lemon
ginger ale

Created for Geoffrey Gelardi, it has a melon and ginger flavour.

Pour all ingredients, except the ginger ale, into a shaker. Shake sharply. Strain into the glass with ice and fill with ginger ale. Stir. Garnish with a slice of kiwi fruit and a wedge of lime on the rim of the glass. Serve with a stirrer.

Hurricane Marilyn

Method : shake
Glass : highball

2cl/2/3oz 54.5 proof Pusser rum
2cl/2/3oz Bacardi
1cl/1/3oz Seagram's V.O. Canadian whisky
1cl/1/3oz Cointreau
7cl/2 1/2oz cranberry juice
7cl/2 1/2oz guava juice
juice of half a lemon
1–2 dashes Grenadine

I created this after arriving in the British Virgin Islands in the Caribbean just after Hurricane Marilyn had devastated the area. What was needed was a powerful antidote for the community to help them forget the misery of the hurricane. It worked.

Pour all ingredients into a shaker and shake sharply. Strain into the glass. Garnish with a sprig of mint set into the top of a fresh strawberry, and a slice of kiwi fruit set on the rim of the glass next to it. This is a friendly, drink to match the personality of the locals. ***Page 105.***

Left
The shimmering GG cocktail.

Right
Lanesborough cocktail.

LADY HUNT

Created for Caroline Hunt, the founder of Rosewood Hotels. The taste is similar to a whisky sour, but more mellow because of the Tia Maria and Amaretto.

Place all of the ingredients into a shaker and shake sharply. Strain into the glass. Garnish with a red Maraschino cherry and a slice of orange. ***Page 175.***

METHOD : shake
GLASS : cocktail

4cl/1 1/2oz malt whisky
1.5cl/1/2oz Tia Maria
1.5cl/1/2oz Amaretto
juice of half a lemon
dash of egg white

LANESBOROUGH

When asked why I moved to this hotel, I say that a bartender is a doctor with the magic ability to cure all – the building had been used as a hospital since the beginning of the 1800s. It is the best place to practise my profession!

Pour the juices and the Grand Marnier into a shaker. Shake sharply, strain into a chilled flute and fill with champagne. Garnish with a fresh strawberry – cut away the stalk and replace it with mint leaves. Sit on the rim of the glass.

METHOD : shake
GLASS : flute

1cl/1/3oz Grand Marnier
2cl/2/3oz passion fruit juice
2cl/2/3oz cranberry juice
champagne

SUMMER SEEN

METHOD : build
GLASS : highball

7cl/2 1/2oz mango juice
7cl/2 1/2oz pineapple juice
2cl/2/3oz lime cordial
1cl/1/3oz fresh lemon juice
4cl/1 1/2oz white rum
1cl/1/3oz blue Curaçao

Pour the pineapple and mango juices, then the lime cordial and lemon juice into the glass. Stir until a yellow/coral colour. In a mixing glass, pour the white rum then add the blue Curaçao to give a blue sky effect. Pour this mixture over the back of a bar spoon so that it floats on top of the fruit juices. Garnish with a slice of star fruit sitting on the rim of a glass. Serve with a stirrer and two straws. ***Page 121.***

VIRGIN LEA

METHOD : blender
GLASS : highball

12cl/4 1/3oz tomato juice
5cl/1 3/4oz passion fruit juice
juice 1/2 a yellow pepper
1 teaspoon clear honey
1–2 dashes
Worcestershire sauce

Right
Virgin Lea (left) and Campari Nobile (right).

A non-alcoholic perfect combination of sharpness, sweetness and spiciness.

Place the yellow pepper, sliced, into the blender and add the juices. Blend for 10 seconds at low speed. Add the honey and the Worcestershire sauce and ice cubes. Blend at high speed for 10 seconds. Strain through a sieve into a jug. Pour into the highball. Garnish with a cherry tomato using a sprig of basil as the stalk. Slice the bottom of the tomato and sit on the rim of the glass. Serve with a straw and a stirrer.

Right
Rick's Café Américain in Casablanca, *1942 – where better to enjoy a champagne cocktail while time goes by.*

INDEX

Acknowledgements

Thanks to my team at The Lanesborough, Fiona Lindsay, Peter Dorelli, Giuliano Morandin, Lynn Bryan, Jim Slavin, Galerie Moderne, IDV (UK) and Prion Books.

Photographic Credits

The publishers would like to acknowledge the following organisations for their kind permission to reproduce the visual material in this book: Allied Domecq 26; Campari 144; Cocktail Culture Collection at Galerie Moderne, London title page, 45, 46, 47, 49; Corbis UK 40, 50; Courvoisier 94; Culver Pictures 42 (bottom); Galliano 159; Guiness Archive 118, Heublein USA 67, 143; Hulton Getty 56, 71; Martini & Rossi 53; Mary Evans Picture Library 23, 65, 113; Moet & Chandon 101; Ronald Grant Archive 58; Savoy Hotel 42 (top); United Distillers (UK) 125, 167; United Kingdom Bartenders Guild Magazine (1936) 25; Veuve Cliquot 6, 96; Vintage Magazine Company 10, 16, 20, 21, 28, 36, 61, 62, 72, 77, 114, 137, 138, 157, 169, 186.

Thanks to the following for glassware:

P. 68, Riedel martini; P. 78, Bohemia Crystal (left) and Christofle (right); P. 81, Tapio by Iattla (centre) and Iona flute by Stuart Crystal (right); P. 86, Bohemia Crystal (left) and Christofle (right); P. 99, Riedel Vinum champagne (left), Symphony by Stuart Crystal (centre) and Flight from Atlantis Crystal (right); P. 105, Ittala Stella highball (centre) and Bohemia Crystal (right); P. 113, Orrefors Intermezzo (left) and Christofle (right); P. 121, Ittala Aarne highball (left), Bohemia Crystal (centre) and Stuart Crystal Symphony (right); P. 128, Daum champagne flute; P. 131, Stuart Crystal Symphony (left) and Christofle champagne flute (right); P. 161, Orrefors Nobel (left) and Bohemia Crystal (right); P. 171, Orrefors Intermezzo (left), Riedel Aquavit (centre); P. 172, Bohemia Crystal; P. 175, Bohemia Crystal (left and right); P. 181, Ittala Tapio; P. 185, Christofle (left and right).